STUD

MW01533041

Prepared by

ELLEN ROSENGARTEN
SINCLAIR COMMUNITY COLLEGE

SOCIOLOGY

Brief Edition

Beth B. Hess
COUNTY COLLEGE OF MORRIS

Elizabeth W. Markson
BOSTON UNIVERSITY

Peter J. Stein
WILLIAM PATTERSON COLLEGE

Macmillan Publishing Company
NEW YORK

Maxwell Macmillan Canada
TORONTO

Maxwell Macmillan International
NEW YORK   OXFORD   SINGAPORE   SYDNEY

Macmillan Publishing Company
866 Third Avenue, New York, New York 10022

Maxwell Macmillan Canada, Inc.
1200 Eglinton Avenue East
Suite 200
Don Mills, Ontario M3C 3N1

ISBN 0-02-403654-4

Printing: 3 4 5 6 7 8   Year: 3 4 5 6 7 8 9 0

TABLE OF CONTENTS

CHAPTER 1
The Sociological Perspective

LEARNING OBJECTIVES

After reading Chapter 1, you should be able to:

1. Understand what sociology studies, the social structures to be examined, and the flexibility we humans have which permits us to adapt to the worlds we create.

2. Summarize the sociological imagination by contrasting troubles which are experienced directly by individuals, and issues, which are caused by factors outside one's own control.

3. List the characteristics of the sociological perspective: a concern for the *totality* of social life, an emphasis on the *context* of human actions, a recognition that *meaning* is a social product, a focus on *collectivity*, and a focus on *interaction*.

4. Discuss the importance of theory and then review the initial roots of sociology by summarizing the work of early thinkers: Comte, Durkheim, Marx, Weber.

5. Compare and contrast the central points of the structural-functional perspective, founded by Talcott Parsons, the conflict perspective, the interpretive perspective, the humanistic perspective, and the feminist perspective.

6. Discuss the major distinctions of two microlevel approaches: the dramaturgical approach and ethnomethodology.

7. Examine biological determinism and individual reductionism as reductionist challenges to the sociological perspective.

8.   Understand how human beings arrive at subjective and objective knowledge and the way sociologists tend to use objective knowledge in research.

9.   Describe what is meant by the scientific method and its major parts: objectivity, precise measurement, and full disclosure of research techniques and results.

10.   List and describe the five steps of the research process.

11.   Describe the major methods sociologists may use to carry out research.

12.   Explain how data may be analyzed by focusing on the importance of percentages, rates and ratios, and measurements of central tendency.

13.   Elaborate the nonscientific factors which may affect the research process.

GLOSSARY CONCEPTS

sociology (p. 2)
social structure (p. 2)
personal troubles (p. 3)
public issues (p. 4)
sociological perspective (p. 4)
collectivity (p. 4)
social facts (p. 4)
social integration (p. 5)
probability (p. 5)
reification (p. 5)
subjective reality (p. 5)
theory (p. 5)
sociology of knowledge (p. 6)
positivism (p. 6)
means of production (p. 7)
Verstehen (p. 7)
functional analysis (p. 9)
institutional shperes (p. 9)
social system (p. 9)
manifest functions (p. 10)
latent functions (p. 10)
dysfunctional patterns (p. 10)
conflict theory (p. 10)
macrosociology (p. 11)

microsociology (p. 11)
interpretive sociology (p. 11)
symbolic interaction (p. 12)
dramaturgical approach (p. 12)
ethnomethodology (p. 13)
reductionism (p. 14)
biological determinism   (p. 14)
sociobiology (p. 14)
exchange and rational-choice models (p. 15)
definition of the situation (p. 17)
scientific method (p. 18)
empirical referents (p. 19)
reliability (p. 19)
validity (p. 19)
replication (p. 19)
sample (p. 19)
qualitative research (p. 20)
quantitative research (p. 20)
variables (p. 22)
constants (p. 22)
hypotheses (p. 22)
independent variables (p. 23)
dependent variables (p. 23)
longitudinal studies (p. 23)

surveys or polls (p. 23)
random sampling (p. 23)
participant observation (p. 24)
secondary analysis (p. 24)
official data (p. 24)
historical records (p. 24)
content analysis (p. 25)
cross-cultural comparison (p. 25)
experiments (p. 26)
field experiments (p. 27)
natural experiments (p. 27)

statistics (p. 27)
percentage (p. 27)
rates (p. 27)
ratio (p. 27)
tendency (p. 28)
mean (p. 28)
median (p. 28)
measures of central mode (p. 28)
particularistic fallacy (p. 29)
tables (p. 29)

REVIEW QUESTIONS

Fill-In Questions

Fill in the blanks in the sentences below with the correct word or items.

1. _____ is the study of human behavior as shaped by group life, including both the collective forces and the ways in which people give meaning to their experiences. (p. 2)

2. The social science which begins with the situation in which behavior takes place is _____. (p. 3)

3. The sociological perspective is based on the assumption that there is a _____ _____ that can be studied in its own right. (p. 6)

4. _____ _____ are patterned, regularities that describe the collectivity rather than its separate parts. (p. 4)

5. _____ was the French sociologist who believed that social facts must be explained by other social facts. (p. 5)

6. The goal of sociologists is to predict the _____ of certain events, rather than dealing with what a specific individual might do. (p. 5)

7. The idea that what we want to know and what we study are social products is the view of the _____ ___ _____. (p. 6)

8.   For Karl Marx, the basic division in society was between _____ and _____-_____ of the means of production. (p. 7)

9.   _____ _____, an early sociologist, saw that technology and modern organizations could become a "new type of prison. (p. 7)

10.   Functionalism examines the parts of society which are called _____ _____: the economy, political system, rules regulating marriage, and family life, eductional processes, and beliefs and rituals. (p. 9)

11.   Robert K. Merton distinguished between _____ functions which referred to intended goals, and _____ functions which referred to unexpected and unintended consequences. (p. 10)

12.   If a behavioral pattern reduces the capacity of the system to adapt and survive, then a functionalist would consider it to be _____. (p. 10)

13.   The _____ perspective views soical order at any moment as the outcome of struggle among groups of unequal power. (pp. 10, 11)

14.   Most humanistic sociologists use the _____ perspective, since this perspective emphasizes the human capacity to resist and change social structures. (p. 13)

15.   A common form of reductionism is _____ _____, which proposes that humans are just apes with bigger brains and have less body hair than the ones in zoos. (p. 14)

16.   The _____ _____ consists of objective observations, precise measurement, and full disclusure of results. (p. 18)

17.   Questionnaires, checklists, and interview forms are all examples of research _____. (p. 19)

18.   Of the two major problems in the use of empirical referents, the one which refers to whether the measuring instrument yields the same results on repeated trials is termed _____. (p. 19)

19.   _____ are factors that differ from one person or collectivity to another. (p. 22)

20.   A difficulty in completing a participant observation is that it may take a long time for the researcher to be _____ by the people being observed. (p. 24)

21. Information collected by others is _____ _____.
(p. 24)

22. Newspapers, magazines, and books often are used as sources for _____
_____. (p. 25)

23. Classic experiments are conducted in a laboratory, while field experiments are conducted in the _____ _____. (p. 27)

24. The proportion or _____ indicates how many of an item there are in every one hundred. (p. 27)

25. If you compared Asians to Hispanics you would be comparing one subpopulation to another and would be using a(n) _____.(p. 27)

26. The three measures of central tendency are the _____, the _____, and the _____. (p. 28)

27. 50 percent of the cases are above the midpoint or _____ and 50 percent are below that number. (p. 28)

28. A(n) _____ _____ occurs when a correlation at the collective level is applied to individuals. (p. 29)

29. A quick glance at a(n) _____ should convey information about the relationships among variables more readily than a detailed description. (p. 29)

30. Deceptions are most obvious in experimental and _____ studies where the people being observed are unaware of the goals of the research. (p. 30)

31. Respondents and _____ can practice deception in research. (p. 31)

True-False Questions

*Circle **T** if the statement below is true. Circle **F** if the statement is false.*

T F 1. The individual is the appropriate unit of analysis for understanding the behavior of Homo sapiens. (p. 2)

T F 2. Considering the sociological imagination, *issues* are private matters, limited to aspects of daily life. (p. 4)

T F 3. Durkheim's notion of social integration meant the rate at which social facts explained change. (p. 5)

T　F　4.　Sociological predictions best apply to groups and categories and less well to individuals and aggregates. (p. 5)

T　F　5.　Sociology has its roots in the Age of Enlightenment. (p. 6)

T　F　6.　Harriet Martineau is best known as the English translator of August Comte. (p. 6)

T　F　7.　The concerns of Max Weber and Karl Marx were fairly similar. (p. 7)

T　F　8.　Women were discouraged during the early years from the field of sociology because they were engaged too frequently in anthropological-type studies. (p. 8)

T　F　9.　Functionalism has been criticized for being conservative and too abstract. (p. 10)

T　F　10.　The conflict perspective focuses on disagreement, and disharmony, but not open hostility among individuals, groups, and system parts. (p. 10)

T　F　11.　An examination of interaction at a personal, face-to-face level is best termed "interpretive." (p. 11)

T　F　12.　When Goffman developed a means to probe to get beneath the meanings of what we take for granted, he engaged in a dramaturgical method. (p. 12)

T　F　13.　Humanist sociologists embrace the notion that sociology should remain value-free. (p. 13)

T　F　14.　Feminist sociologists have been instrumental in recognizing that gender is an element of social structure. (p. 13)

T　F　15.　A criticism of the exchange model is that people do not always act out of self-interest. (p. 15)

T　F　16.　Subjective knowledge tells us directly about broad social systems which affect behavior. (p. 18)

T　F　17.　Some sociological methods can totally eliminate researcher bias. (p. 18)

T　F　18.　*Qualitative* studies are generally viewed as more scientific and rigorous than quantitative studies. (p. 20)

T　F　19.　A theory is a conceptual model of how social life is constructed. (p. 22)

T　F　20.　The independent variable comes first in the chain of events and its typical characteristics are given rather than chosen. (p. 23)

T　F　21.　Cross-sectional studies take place only at one time while longitudinal studies take place over time. (p. 23)

T　F　22.　The amount and quality of information gathered depend on the respondent's willingness to answer. (p. 23)

T   F   23.   Pilot research studies typically use large representative samples (p. 24)

T   F   24.   A limitation of secondary analysis is that it is quite expensive in terms of time and money. (p. 24)

T   F   25.   In a classic experiment the independent variable, or causal factor, is introduced into the experimental group. (p 26)

T   F   26.   If a sociologist studies a community before and after the passage of a tough antipornography law, then that research has used a natural experiment. (p. 27)

T   F   27.   The simplest and most important statistic is a ratio. (p. 27)

T   F   28.   If a researcher is concerned that data might be misused, the researcher may choose to interpret that data as narrowly as possible. (p. 28)

T   F   29.   Data speak for themselves. (p. 28)

T   F   30.   The numbers in each part of the body of the table are called cells. (p. 29)

Matching Questions

Match the items in Column B with the correct answer in Colunm A (columns continue on next page).

COLUMN A	COLUMN B
1. Emile Durkheim (p. 5)	a. An aggregate, category, or group.
2. social facts (p. 4)	b. Totality of social life, context, meaning is a social product, focus on collectivity and interaction.
3. theory (p. 5)	c. Birth rates and death rates are examples of an idea for which Emile Durkheim laid the groundwork which are patterned realities that describe the collectivity.
4. collectivity (p. 4)	
5. characteristics of the sociological perspective (p. 6)	d. A set of logically related statements that explain an entire class of events.
6. August Comte (p. 6)	e. This early sociologist founded sociology and believed in positivism.
7. ethnomethodology (p. 13)	f. This early sociologist believed social order always is uncertain because it is based on exploitation and conflict.
8. functionalism (p. 9)	g. This early sociologist wanted to establish sociology as a separate academic discipline and placed an emphasis on the study of society rather than on individuals.
9. Karl Marx (p. 6)	
10. deciding what to study (p. 21)	

| COLUMN A | COLUMN B |

COLUMN A

11. validity (p. 19)

12. survey (p. 23)

13. secondary analysis (p. 24)

14. field experiment (p. 27)

15. cross-cultural comparison (p. 25)

16. random sampling (p. 23)

17. empirical referents (p. 19)

18. replication (p. 19)

19. experiment (p. 26)

20. professional journals (p. 28)

21. mean (p. 28)

22. statistics (p. 27)

23. mode (p. 28)

COLUMN B

h. The central focus of this perspective is between two levels of social reality: the whole and the parts of society.

i. A way to dig beneath reality to discover the basic meaning of social action developed by Garfinkel.

j. Items that can be measured and counted.

k. Involves repeating a specific study with different respondents, in various settings, and at other time periods.

l. All possible respondents have an equal chance of being chosen.

m. A method found more commonly in psychology that in sociology.

n. Refers to whether the measuring instrument is really measuring what it was designed to.

o. The most nonscientific step in the research process.

p. A poll which yields data from a large group of respondents.

q. The generality of sex-linked behaviors is favorite topic.

r. The least used method by sociologists, but the closest to the scientific ideal.

s. An arithmetical average.

t. Official data and historical records are examples.

u. A way sociologists communicate with one another.

v. "Candid Camera" is a good example of this method.

w. The single most common category of cases.

x. Numerical techniques for the classification and analysis of data.

ANSWERS
Answers to Fill-In Questions

1. sociology
2. sociology
3. collective reality
4. social facts
5. Durkheim
6. probability
7. sociology of knowledge
8. owners; non-owners
9. Max Weber
10. institutional spheres
11. manifest; latent
12. dysfunctional
13. conflict
14. interpretive
15. biological determinism
16. scientific method

17. instruments
18. reliability
19. variables
20. accepted
21. secondary analysis
22. content analysis
23. real world
24. percentage
25. ratio
26. mean; median; mode
27. median
28. particularistic fallacy
29. table
30. observational
31. researchers

Answers to True-False Questions

1.	F	9.	F	17.	F	25.	T
2.	F	10.	F	18.	F	26.	T
3.	F	11.	T	19.	T	27.	F
4.	F	12.	F	20.	T	28.	T
5.	T	13.	T	21.	T	29.	F
6.	T	14.	T	22.	T	30.	T
7.	T	15.	T	23.	F		
8.	T	16.	F	24.	F		

Answers to Matching Questions

1.	g	9.	f	17.	j
2.	c	10.	o	18.	k
3.	d	11.	n	19.	r
4.	a	12.	p	20.	u
5.	b	13.	t	21.	s
6.	e	14.	v	22.	x
7.	i	15.	q	23.	w
8.	h	16.	l		

EXERCISE #1

The difference between sociology and psychology is often difficult to appreciate at first glance. With this idea in mind, think about the following situation.

Rap music has become a popular aspect of the American music scene, just as blues, jazz, swing, and rock & roll are. MTV has aired many rap music videos and some radio stations regularly play the music of the Fresh Prince, 2 Live Crew, N.W.A., Public Enemy, the Beastie Boys, 3rd Brass, and other groups. Rap primarily has been the music of young black men, although there are a growing number of women and whites recording the music. Some of the music has a political message, while other themes revolve around rage, sex, racism, generational differences, and social conditions, but most contain harsh language which certain people in our society find objectionable. Some argue rap is a safety value, a kind of positive response to miserable experiences. Others find rap insulting, obscene, violent, and/or scary.

1. You are a psychologist who must see the son of parents who are concerned about their teenager's fascination with rap music.

    A. How would you explain rap to the parents?

    B. What psychological questions might the parents raise? Name at least three.

        1.

        2.

        3.

2. Amanda Gruber is a sociologist who does not know much about rap, how or when it arose in society, how different people react to the lyrics or music, and how the music is viewed by various segments of the population.

    A. If you were Amanda, what sociological questions would you raise? List at least five.

        1.

        2.

3.

4.

5.

B. Briefly explain rap music from the sociological viewpoint that Amanda Gruber will take.

EXERCISE #2

Early in the Spring of 1990, the governor of Idaho, Cecil Andrus, vetoed what would have become this nation's most restrictive abortion law. That law would have banned abortion for nearly every reason a woman could have for seeking this procedure including rape or incest. The bill was patterned after a National Right to Life model that other states in the past have rejected on the grounds that it was too restrictive. Under the now vetoed bill, abortions performed would target physicians with civil penalties of up to $10,000 for a first offense, $30,000 for a second offense, and $50,000 for each additional violation. Women who sought the procedure would not have been held legally responsible. Anti-abortion groups had hoped to use the Idaho law to challenge the U.S. Supreme Court's commitment to legalized abortion.

Pretend you are a functionalist, then a sociologist who uses the conflict model, and last a sociologist using the interpretative models. Recall that all three models try to answer the question, "How is society possible?"

A   1. As a *functionalist*, what major question(s) would you raise? (Remember the functionalist's questions which ask, "What are the consequences of a given social pattern? How does it meet human needs and preserve the group as a whole?") What, exactly, makes your question(s) functionalist?

    2. How would you, as a functionalist, explain the abortion dilemma?

B   1. You are now taking the *conflict* perspective. What major question(s) will you raise? (The conflict perspective questions include, "Who benefits from any given social arrangement?") Why is/are your question(s) uniquely "conflict"?

    2. How would you, from this perspective, explain the abortion dilemma?

C   1. Now you are using the *interpretive* perspectives. With the *symbolic interactive* perspective, what major question(s) need to be raised? (This perspective asks, "How do people make sense of their world, influence one another, and define themselves?") Exactly what makes your question(s) within the interpretive tradition?

    2. As a symbolic interactionist, how would you explain the abortion dilemma?

EXERCISE #3

Many cities in the United States have experienced what the media calls, "drug wars." In a medium-sized midwestern city, local citizens who felt fairly immune from the drug-related problems of larger cities, were jolted to realize the drug problem was literally in their backyards. On six separate occasions, different houses were sprayed with bullets from cars. Children and adults had to run to escape injury. The mayor issued stern warnings that drive-by shootings would not be tolerated and some community leaders blamed the police chief for the continued shooting of homes. Newspaper accounts of the history of drug dealing, arrests for drugs in the affected neighborhoods, and police efforts keep the story front page news.

1. Begin by describing your own attitudes, expectations or values, in investigating this situation.

2. What, exactly, could be measured? Circle what you would be interested in measuring and explain why. Put a check by what captures your interest.

3. List three empirical referents.

    a.

    b.

    c.

4. Who is your population?

CHAPTER 2
Culture

LEARNING OBJECTIVES

After reading Chapter 2, you should be able to:

1. Understand the unique flexibility and adaptability of the human animal.

2. Understand the evolutionary basis of culture, and trace how culture emerged.

3. Explain the nature of culture, how sociologists describe culture, and why it is a blueprint for living.

4. Explain why symbols are the key to culture and how humans communicate through symbols.

5. Discuss the uniqueness of human communication, the types of communications, and how language shapes human thought (the Spair-Whorf hypothesis).

6. Sketch out the six types of cultures and societies: gathering, hunting, herding, horticulture, agriculture, and industrialization.

7. Understand how sociologists analyze culture in terms of cultural universals and cultural variability.

8. Compare and contrast ethnocentrism and cultural relativism.

9. Distinguish between ideal and real culture.

10. Distinguish the various classifications of norms and relate them to the values.

11. Compare and contrast subcultures and countercultures.

12. Relate the core values of the American ethos to our ideas about the work ethic.

13. Define the nature of popular culture.

14. Describe the process involved in the production of culture.

15. Examine the role of the mass media as principal channels of communication in a mass society.

16. Review the effects of the mass media by focusing on the impact the media have on attitudes and behaviors.

17. Review trends in protest music and specify what genres speak to what segments of society.

18. Define sports and differentiate the nature, parameters, and characteristics of amateur and professional sports, especially as this impacts college and high school athletics.

GLOSSARY CONCEPTS

foraging (p. 38)
gathering (p. 38)
culture (p. 38)
artifacts (p. 38)
symbol (p. 38)
kinesics (p. 40)
mode of subsistence (p. 41)
preliterate (p. 42)
historical (p. 42)
cultural universals (p. 45)
cultural variability (p. 45)
ethnocentrism (p. 46)
cultural relativism (p. 47)
ideal culture (p. 49)
real culture (p. 49)
social norms (p. 49)
folkways (p. 50)

sanctions (p. 50)
mores (p. 50)
laws (p. 50)
values (p. 51)
rituals (p. 51)
rites of passage (p. 51)
subcultures (p. 52)
jargons (p. 53)
countercultures (p. 53)
cultural heterogeneity (p. 54)
American ethos (p. 54)
work ethic (p. 55)
conspicuous consumption (p. 56)
cultural or ideological hegemony (p. 56)
popular culture (p. 60)
mass culture (p. 61)
production of popular culture (p. 61)

REVIEW QUESTIONS

Fill-In Questions

Fill in the blanks in the sentences below with the correct word or item.

1. Human behavior is not determined by instinct; instead it is characterized by flexibility and _____. (p. 37)

2. The basic group of _____ consisted of a female and her children who foraged to survive. (p. 38)

3. Tools, ideals and values, and solutions to the problems of survival make up _____. (p. 38)

4. All human communication is _____. (p. 39)

5. The more elaborate the _____ _____ _____, the greater the consequent differences among people and groups within a society. (p. 42)

6. Societies without written language are _____, whereas societies with written records are referred to as _____. (p. 42)

7. The division of labor in societies which developed hunting typically meant _____ hunted, while _____ continued to forage and gather. (p. 42)

8. The use of a plow and the irrigation of crops, which ensures a dependable food supply, is descriptive of _____ societies. (p. 43)

9. Formal _____ and the interdependencies of a complex division of labor hold agricultural societies together. (p. 43)

10. Cultural _____ are basic elements found in every culture. (p. 45)

11. Ideal culture refers to what people feel "ought to be," while _____ culture refers to actual behavior. (p. 49)

12. Violations of _____ are usually handled informally. (p. 50)

13. Laws are enforced by _____ sanctions which are exercised by officials specifically charged with maintaining order. (p. 50)

14. Laws are designed to ensure public order but often reflect _____ culture. (p. 51)

15. When a boy undergoes a ceremony which marks him as a man, sociologists say he is taking part in a(n) _____ _____ _____. (p. 51)

16. In the U.S. religious, racial, and ethnic minorities have developed _____ that permit them to survive under conditions different from those faced by the dominant group. (p. 53)

17. Countercultures differ from subcultures in that countercultures are in _____ to existing social patterns. (p. 53)

18. The fifteen core values that Robin Williams identified comprise the American _____. (p. 53)

19. Work as "calling," success as a sign of grace, and individuals as monitors of their own state of grace are elements of the _____ _____. (p. 55)

20. An idea that produces some ambivalence today, _____ _____ refers to lavish displays of wastefulness designed to impress others. (p. 56)

21. The control over the production of values and norms by those in power is known as _____ _____. (p. 56)

22. The two aspects of popular culture are: _____ and the needs of an advanced _____ to generate new markets. (p. 60)

23. Leisure-time pursuits reduce _____ and _____. (p. 60)

24. Since play is an end in and of itself, it is said to be _____. (p. 61)

25. _____ _____ creates common values and attitudes in a large, heterogeneous society. (p. 61)

26. _____ _____ is the outcome of interaction among the objects produced, the profit-making producers and distributors of those products, and the social groups that consume them. (p. 61)

27. The condition that makes mass culture possible is _____ _____. (p. 61)

28. The two most common leisure activities in the United States are _____ _____ and _____ _____. (p. 62)

29. Most research on the effects of mass media has focused on the potential viewing of televised _____. (p. 62)

30. Viewing television can stimulate _____ development among children. (p. 62)

31. The music industry is stratified by _____. (p. 64)

32. Sports differ from _____ in that sports are organized by sets of rules. (p. 64)

33. In the United States today _____ sports are associated with working-class activities that are organized at a community level. (p. 64, 65)

True-False Questions

*Circle **T** if the statement below is true. Circle **F** if the statement is false.*

T   F   1. Human groups can survive without culture if they can develop a technology that enables them to obtain food. (p. 38)

T   F   2. Human nature exists and develops independently of culture. (p. 38)

T   F   3. The most important symbol system is language which is socially defined. (p. 39)

T   F   4. While language must be learned and is culturally based, all nonverbal communication, or gesture, is inborn and the meanings are not rooted in culture. (p. 39)

T   F   5. The care and herding of animals is typical of horticultural societies. (p. 43)

T   F   6. Industrialization is associated with complex knowledge, technology, and material culture. (p. 43)

T   F   7. There is conclusive evidence that the former Philippine government exploited the Tasaday as a public-relations gimmick. (p. 45)

T   F   8. Even though culture is an abstraction, parts and elements of culture can be seen and touched. (p. 43)

T   F   9. Ethnocentrism can become dysfunctional when it leads to hostility. (p. 46)

T   T   10. Elements and parts of cultures should be understood by the standards of another culture. (p. 47)

T   T   11. The mores of one historical period are the mores of another because mores do not change over time. (p. 50)

T   T   12. Enacted laws go against previously accepted behaviors and reflect real culture. (p. 50)

T   T   13. There is a direct cultural link between norms and values. (p. 51)

T   T   14.   Subcultures appear wherever access to the general culture is different for some segments of the population than for others. (p. 52)

T   T   15.   The idea of a work ethic was originally described by Max Weber as the Protestant Ethic. (p. 55)

T   T   16.   According to the early capitalists, failure in life was due to exploitation in the workplace. (p. 56)

T   T   17.   Conspicuous consumption is an idea handed down to us from our Puritan forebears who developed the work ethos. (p. 56)

T   T   18.   Ideas and things are cultural artifacts. (p. 56)

T   T   19.   Caring, openness, and cooperation are values from the 1980s and are embraced by yuppies. (p. 57)

T   T   20.   Leisure time is allocated and structured by political and economic forces. (p. 61)

T   T   21.   The production of mass culture is socially structured. (p. 61)

T   T   22.   Throughout most of the world, media are owned by private corporations. (p. 61)

T   T   23.   Owners of media influence the content of what we see and read, often with a particular political purpose in mind. (p. 62)

Matching Questions

Match the items in Column B with the correct answer in Column A (columns continue on next page).

COLUMN A	COLUMN B
1. customary laws (p. 50)	a. Members share a given territory and language, feel responsibile for one another and recognize their shared identity.
2. cultural heterogeneity (p.54)	
	b. The study of nonverbal communication.
3. cultural variability (p. 45)	c. Norms that are formally adopted and govern behavior most essential to group survival and apply to all members of a society.
4. laws (p. 50)	
	d. An example would be brushing your teeth in the morning.
5. jargon (p. 53)	
	e. An oppositional lifestyle of those who cannot or will not conform to the dominant norms.
6. ideal culture (p. 49)	
7. subcultures (p. 52)	f. The specialized language of physicians, lawyers, or garbage collectors.

COLUMN A

8.   symbol (p. 38)

9.   rituals (p.51)

10. folkways (p. 50)

11. ethnocentrism (p. 46)

12. social norms (p. 49)

13. counterculture (p. 53)

14. culture (p. 38)

15. values (p. 51)

16. core values (p. 54)

17. mores (p. 50)

18. cultural relativism (p. 47)

19. kinesics (p. 40)

20. mass culture (p. 61)

21. sports (p. 64)

22. punk rock, heavy metal, and rap (p. 64)

23. mass media (p. 62)

24. popular culture (p. 60)

25. fear and hatred of women and homosexuals (p. 64)

COLUMN B

g.   An effort to understand the world as seen by members of other societies.

h.   Rules of behavior.

i.   The highest virtues and standards of a society.

j.   These norms are crucial to social order and cover moral behavior.

k.   Central beliefs about what is important.

l.   The variety of customs, beliefs, and artifacts devised by humans to meet universal needs.

m.   An object, event, or sound that signifies nothing in and of itself, but only the purely arbitrary meaning that members of a group attach to it.

n.   The belief that a person's own culture is the best and the consequent judging of other cultures by that standard.

o.   Crystallization of traditional practices which make clear what is acceptable and the penalties for disobedience.

p.   These surround important lifecycle events like birth, death, and marriage.

q.   The more complex the culture, the more diverse the population, the more of these you will find in a society.

r.   The existence of many different subgroups and subcultures in a society.

s.   Material comfort, equality, achievement and success are a few examples.

t.   These test the limits of culturally permissible sound and lyrics.

u.   Consists of what people do in their leisure time and the products designed for mass consumption.

v.   What rap music and heavy metal have in common.

w.   The channels of communication in a mass society, primarily the print and electric media.

x.   Elements of popular culture that are produced and distributed through the mass media.

y.   Embodies the values of work, competition, manliness, and commercialism.

ANSWERS

Answers to Fill-In Questions

1. adaptability
2. prehumans
3. culture
4. symbolic
5. division of labor
6. preliterate; historical
7. men; women
8. agricultural
9. laws
10. universals
11. real
12. folkways
13. formal
14. ideal
15. rite of passage
16. subcultures
17. opposition
18. ethos
19. work ethic
20. conspicuous consumption
21. ideological or cultural hegemony
22. play; economy
23. anxiety; tension
24. expressive
25. mass culture
26. production of culture
27. mass media
28. watching television; reading newspapers
29. violence
30. cognitive
31. race
32. play
33. amateur

Answers to True-False Questions

1.	F	11.	F	21.	T
2.	F	12.	F	22.	F
3.	T	13.	F	23.	T
4.	F	14.	T		
5.	F	15.	T		
6.	T	16.	F		
7.	F	17.	F		
8.	F	18.	T		
9.	T	19.	F		
10.	F	20.	T		

Answers to Matching Questions

1.	o	8.	m	15.	k	22.	t
2.	r	9.	p	16.	y	23.	w
3.	1	10.	d	17.	j	24.	u
4.	c	11.	n	18.	g	25.	v
5.	f	12.	h	19.	b		
6.	i	13.	e	20.	x		
7.	q	14.	a	21.	y		

EXERCISE #1

On April 30, 1970, President Nixon announced U.S. troops had crossed the South Vietnam border and entered Cambodia. That announcement triggered anti-war demonstrations on many college campuses throughout the country. Kent State University, in northeastern Ohio, was no exception. Demonstrations took place on- and off-campus. A state of emergency was declared which closed bars in the small downtown areas of Kent, Ohio, and former Governor James Rhodes was asked to send in the National Guard. The Guard stayed in tents on the campus and were cursed and had rocks thrown at them during a demonstration by students on Monday, May 4, 1970. The Guard had used tear gas the previous day to break up students on the Commons and again used tear gas May 4 to force demonstrators to an athletic practice field. Of the 116 Guardsmen who were marching up Blanket Hill on the Kent State campus, twenty-eight turned and fired their weapons. Most students were staying seventy-five feet away from the Guards. Eight of the twenty-eight Guards claimed later they fired toward the students; the others said they fired their rifles into the air. No Guardsman was ever convicted of a crime nor was any public official. Four students died.

1.   Identify four norms.

    1.

    2.

    3.

    4.

2.   Explain how traditional values clashed with values developed during the 1960s.

EXERCISE #2

Review pages 54, 55, and 56 which describe the work ethic. Think about the work ethic as it has subtly affected your life, values, and attitudes.

1.   How did you learn such lessons as "strive to be successful," "save your money," and "work hard"? Relate a specific example for each of these "lessons."

"strive to be successful":

"save your money":

"work hard":

"be the best you can be"

2.   How does your choice of a major fit in with the work ethic?

3.   Describe how advertisements for products on television or in magazines promote the work ethic. Describe the advertisement, name the product, and then explain how the work ethic is promoted.

Advertisement	Product Name	Explanation

4. In thinking about your own life, in what ways, small or large, have you (or your family) been materialistic? Be very specific.

5. Can you think of any instances in which you, your family members, or friends have displayed conspicuous consumption? If you cannot think of an example from your own experiences, use one from a television drama.

EXERCISE #3

Investigate the relationship between play and games by examining ads over the past year in your local newspaper. Locate a minimum of three different advertisements for three different types of "play" and games. Clip each ad neatly and attach them to this exercise.

1. For each ad, describe the location in your community where the activity takes place.

Advertisement #1	Description of play or game	Location

Advertisement #2	Description of play or game	Location

Advertisement #3	Description of play or game	Location

EXERCISE #4

Listen to music from the 1960s, 1970s, and 1980s. You can choose radio stations which play "oldies," those which play contemporary recordings, and MTV.

1.   Compare major themes in the lyrics.

1960s

	Song Title	Type of Music	Theme	Artist or Group
1.				
2.				
3.				

1970s

	Song Title	Type of Music	Theme	Artist or Group
1.				
2.				
3.				

1980s

	Song Title	Type of Music	Theme	Artist or Group
1.				
2.				
3.				

2. What major themes can you see emerging from each decade?

3.   How are women portrayed in the 1960s, 1970s, 1980s?

   1960s

   1970s

   1980s

4.   What role(s) are men seen to play?

5.   What changes do you see in the recording artist or group over a twenty-year period?

CHAPTER 3
Social Structures, Groups, and Interaction

LEARNING OBJECTIVES

After reading Chapter 3, you should be able to:

1. Understand the role of social structure in society and how it fits with culture.

2. Differentiate status and role and explain how norms, status, and roles make social life predictable.

3. Examine the components of social structure from the conflict and functionalist approaches by discussing the part of social system micro- and macrosystems, status, and role.

4. Explain role conflict and strain and how to reduce them.

5. Explain the definition of the situation and how that relates to status, role, and new situations.

6. Summarize the characteristics of a group.

7. Distinguish primary from secondary groups and the behaviors which characterize them.

8. Contrast the nature of the relationships in *Gemeinschaft* and *Gesellschaft* societies.

9. Distinguish among in-groups, out-groups, and reference groups, and relate the influence these groups generate in our lives.

10.   Explain group structure in terms of how groups are formed, their influence, size, and social networks.

11.   Describe each type of interaction process and explain how each mode is related.

12.   Understand how the dramaturgical view analyzes interaction.

13.   Examine ways emotions are socially constructed and maintained.

14.   Define formal organization and then show how bureaucracy is a type of formal organization.

15.   List the positive and negative features of bureaucracy.

GLOSSARY CONCEPTS

social structure (p. 70)
norms (p. 70)
status (p. 70)
role (p. 70)
social system (p. 71)
ascribed statuses (p. 73)
achieved statuses (p. 73)
master status (p. 73)
status set (p. 73)
role prescriptions (p. 73)
role conflict (p. 74)
role strain (p. 74)
definition of the situation (p. 75)
anomie (p. 75)
group (p. 76)
primary group (p. 77)
expressive behavior (p. 77)
secondary groups (p. 77)
instrumental behavior (p. 78)
Gemeinschaft (p. 78)
Gesellschaft (p. 78)
in-groups (p. 79)
out-groups (p. 79)
reference groups (p. 79)
sociogram (p. 80)

dyad (p. 80)
triad (p. 80)
social network (p. 81)
interaction processes (p. 81)
task or instrumental role (p. 82)
expressive roles (p. 82)
dramaturgical view (p. 83)
frontstage interaction (p. 83)
backstage interaction (p. 83)
principles of exchange (p. 83)
coercion (p. 84)
competition (p. 84)
cooperation (p. 84)
compromise (p. 85)
conflict (p. 85)
cooptation (p. 87)
mediation (p. 87)
ritualized release of hostility (p. 87)
sociology of emotions (p. 87)
feeling rules (p. 87)
formal organizations (p. 88)
social institution (p. 89)
burequcracy (p. 89)
informal primary groups (p. 92)

REVIEW QUESTIONS

Fill-In Questions

Fill in the blanks in the sentences below with the correct word or item.

1. The components of _____ _____ include systems, norms, statuses, roles, interactions, and groups. (p. 70)

2. The dynamic aspect of a status which deals with expected behavior is a(n) _____. (p. 70)

3. Microsystem refers to _____-_____-_____ interaction while macrosystem is a social system at a higher level of abstraction. (p. 72)

4. Statuses over which we have little or no control are _____, but statuses we earn through merit, choice, or effort are _____. (p. 73)

5. All of the statuses you occupy is a(n) _____ _____. (p. 73)

6. The flexibility you have in playing a role is limited by your multiple _____. (p. 74)

7. The situation when two or more statuses have incompatible demands or expectations is _____ _____. (p. 74)

8. The _____ of the situation is a process by which people interpret and evaluate the social context. (p. 75)

9. The collection of people bound together by a distinctive set of shared social relationship is a(n) _____. (p. 76)

10. In a(n) _____ group, members have warm, initimate, personal ties with one another, whereas _____ groups have few emotional ties to one another. (p. 77)

11. *Gemeinschaft* exists in communities with many _____ group relationships. (p. 78)

12. Strong in-group and out-group feelings reinforce _____. (p. 79)

13. Group structure can be studied through the _____ which identifies interaction patterns. (p. 80)

14. The _____ is more stable than the dyad, even though there may be less affection and intimacy evident. (p. 84)

15. Role _____ describe the division of labor in social relationships and differ in content and complexity. (p. 82)

16. The _____ view of interaction sees all role partners as actors performing roles in a social setting. (p. 83)

17. _____ interaction occurs in full view of the public whereas _____ interaction is free of public performance constraints. (p. 83)

18. Except for _____, the use of force to induce compliance, all other interaction processes are characterized by some degree of willingness to follow the norms. (p. 84)

19. A(n) _____ is a cooperative effort to minimize the all or nothing aspects of competition. (p. 85)

20. The three ways to reduce conflict are: cooptation, _____, and ritualized release of hostility. (pp. 85, 86)

21. When people who had been dissenting have a stake in the peaceful settlement of a conflict, _____ has occured. (p. 87)

22. Emotions are constructed within a cultural and _____ context. (p. 87)

23. _____ are social structures characterized by formality, ranked positions, large size, relative complexity, and long duration. (p. 88)

24. The sum of formal organizations of society is its _____ _____. (p. 89)

25. A type of formal organization common in modern societies is the _____, a formal organization characterized by rationality and efficiency. (p. 89)

26. The _____ _____ describes how incompetence is rewarded in the bureaucracy. (pp. 90, 91)

27. A negative feature of bureaucracy is _____ Law which says work expands to fill the number of hours allotted to it. (p. 91)

True-False Questions

*Circle **T** if the statement is true. Circle **F** if the statement is false.*

T   F   1.   Most social behavior is orderly and predictable. (p. 70)

T   F   2.   One reason the concept of social structure may be hard to understand is that we often try to find causes for behavior within ourselves rather than in external sources. (pp. 70, 71)

T   F   3.   When statuses are more or less in harmony with each other they are said to be consistent.   (p. 73)

T   F   4.   Because we participate in a number of social systems, we can occupy very few statuses. (p. 72)

T   F   5.   A way to reduce role strain is to redesign one's role set, and strive for status consistency. (p. 75)

T   F   6.   People find they cannot tolerate anomie. (p. 75)

T   F   7.   The family is our first primary group. (p. 77)

T   F   8.   Secondary groups are often formed within primary settings. (p. 78)

T   F   9.   Both *Gemeinschaft* and *Gesellschaft* elements can exist together in simple societies. (p. 78)

T   F   10.   The amount of hostility directed toward out-groups is related to the strength of reference groups. (p. 79)

T   F   11.   Of all groups, the dyad is the most fragile, for it can be destroyed so easily. (pp. 80)

T   F   12.   Size is related to interaction in groups. (p. 80)

T   F   13.   The composition of a person's social network remains fixed throughout a lifetime. (p. 81)

T   F   14.   Behavior in groups is spontaneous and often unstructured. (p. 81)

T   F   15.   The class "clown" is fulfilling an expressive role. (pp. 82, 83)

T   F   16.   According to Goffman's dramaturgical view, the roles we play make up a social script. (p. 83)

T   F   17.   Giving gifts is a way of establishing and maintaining social relationships. (p. 84)

T   F   18.   Compromise, cooperation, and competition are all modes of exchange. (p. 84)

T   F   19.   Competition is the most social mode of interaction according to the exchange perspective and the one which is the basis of social order. (p. 85)

T   F   20.   The use of a third party to resolve disputes, as in a divorce, is an example of the ritualized release of hostility. (p. 87)

T   F   21.   Emotions are shaped by social interactions. (p. 88)

T   F   22.   Shared emotions provide a basis for social cohesion. (p. 88)

T   F   23.   Only preschoolers and adults who work at home are exempt from formal organizations. (p. 88)

T   F   24.   Formal organizations are larger but less structured than smaller groups. (p. 89)

T   F   25.   A description of the purest form of bureaucracy is the ideal type. (p. 89)

T   F   26.   Discouragement of favoritism and a clear chain of command are positive aspects of the bureaucracy. (p.89, 90)

T   F   27.   The impersonal patterns of relationships within bureaucracies give rise to informal primary groups among workers. (p. 92)

Matching Questions

Match the items in Column B with the correct answer in Column A (columns continue on next page).

COLUMN A

1. characteristics of a group (p. 76)
2. feeling rules (p. 87)
3. anomie (p. 75)
4. cooperation (p. 84)
5. in-group (p. 79)
6. competition (p. 84)
7. social system (p. 71)
8. instrumental roles (p. 82)
9. *Gesellschaft* (p. 78)
10. dyad (p. 80)
11. social structure (p. 70)
12. master status (p. 73)
13. social network (p. 81)
14. conflict (p. 82)
15. interaction processes (p. 81)

COLUMN B

a. Position in a social system.

b. This group influences your identity, norms, and values whether or not you actually belong to it.

c. Comprised of the patterns of social interaction through which culture is made possible; the patterns of relationship within which behavior is carried out.

d. This is comprised of the sum total of a person's group memberships and relationships.

e. Contractual relationships where social bonds are voluntary, based on rational self-interest.

f. Interaction that occurs when people try to destroy or disable their opponents.

g. The groups to which "we" belong.

h. The most important status we occupy, and the one that affects almost every aspect of your life.

i. The sharing of resources in order to achieve a common goal.

j. The ways in which partners agree on the goals, negotiate how to reach the goal, and the distribute resources.

k. An arrangement of statuses and roles that exist apart from the people occupying them.

l. Roles oriented toward specific goals.

16. reference group (p. 79)

17. status (p. 70)

m. Characterized by intimacy, total involvement, and joint responsibility.

n. The situation in which norms are absent, unclear, or confusing.

o. These shape how, when, with whom, and where an emotion is expressed.

p. Results when situations are defined as ones in which scarce resources will go to some or are unequally distributed.

q. A sense of membership, interdependence, a distinctive set of social relationships, a feeling that the behaviors of each is relevant to everyone else.

ANSWERS

Answers to Fill-In Questions

1.	social structure	15.	structures
2.	role	16.	dramaturgical
3.	face-to-face	17.	frontstage; backstage
4.	ascribed; achieved	18.	coercion
5.	status set	19.	compromise
6.	statuses	20.	mediation
7.	role conflict	21.	cooptation
8.	definition	22.	historical
9.	group	23.	complex organizations
10.	primary; secondary	24.	social institutions
11.	primary	25.	bureaucracy
12.	competition	26.	Peter Principle
13.	sociogram	27.	Parkinson's
14.	triad		

Answers to True-False Questions

1.	T	10.	F	19.	F
2.	T	11.	T	20.	F
3.	T	12.	T	21.	T
4.	F	13.	F	22.	T
5.	F	14.	F	23.	T
6.	T	15.	T	24.	F
7.	T	16.	T	25.	T
8.	F	17.	T	26.	T
9.	F	18.	T	27.	T

Answers to Matching Questions

1.	q	7.	k	13.	d
2.	o	8.	l	14.	f
3.	n	9.	e	15.	j
4.	i	10.	m	16.	b
5.	g	11.	c	17.	a
6.	p	12.	h		

EXERCISE #1

Lindsey is a twenty-six year old secretary who is divorced, has a high school diploma, and is the mother of a preschool-aged daughter, Megan. She is very close to her family and depends on her sisters and mother for occasional loans, meals, and babysitting. Lindsey's father, whom she idolized, died two years ago unexpectedly from a heart attack. Lindsey struggles to make ends meet on her secretarial salary but often is "short" before payday. Typical suppers for her and her daughter are canned soup and crackers.

Lindsey takes occasional college courses with the vague idea of being "something other than a secretary" but finding the money to pay for the courses is hard. She also feels guilty about being away from her daughter during the evening hours. Lindsey's social activities revolve around her church. Lindsey's ex-husband, Thomas, has remarried, and has their daughter with him and his new family every other weekend. Thomas does not spend much time with Megan on those weekends and never takes Megan to church, despite Lindsey's instructions. Instead, he usually leaves Megan with his new wife, Anne, or with his parents, who adore Megan.

Megan's paternal grandparents always are eager to be with their granddaughter and make it very easy for Thomas to drop the girl off at their home. These grandparents schedule their vacations around Megan and her interests. Lindsey complains that Megan is shamefully "spoiled" when she visits these grandparents and that straightening the child out when the visits end is hard on both of them. Lindsey resents Thomas' dumping Megan off on Anne or his parents and feels Thomas ought to spend time with his daughter. Megan has acted out at her daycare center.

1. Reread "Systems Theory at Work—The Genogram," page 74. Then construct a genogram for Lindsey's family.

2.   Lindsey is seeing a family therapist to help her understand her ex-husband's behavior, why the grandparents spoil Megan, and why Megan is confused and acting out at daycare. After looking at the genogram you constructed, explain how a systems perspective specialist would view Lindsey's problems.

3.   What linkages can you discover between microsystem information and macrosystem information?

Microsystem information   **Macrosystem information**

EXERCISE #2

Carl is a thirty-eight year-old mathematician who is employed by a large corporation. He is in charge of a department which is responsible for the development and implementation of automatic bank teller machines. He frequently travels across the country when a sudden problem with the machines occurs. He is married to Toni who is a high school social studies teacher. Carl and Toni have two young children. Toni coaches the tennis team at the high school and, in the evenings and summers, at a local tennis court.

Carl's sudden business trips frequently cause problems for Toni with her busy schedule. If these trips occur when Toni has a commitment to teach a tennis lesson, a sitter must be found for the children, who express fears or resentment when both their parents are gone. Sitters the children like are not easy to find. When the children, who are five and seven years old, are particularly resentful that their parents are out for the evening, they give the sitters a hard time. Their behavior has narrowed the number of sitters who will stay with them, and causes Toni some guilt about leaving for her "moonlighting" job.

Toni feels she must keep up her second job so that her family can maintain its lifestyle and afford a few extras that they all enjoy. Carl cannot reduce the number of trips he makes or the hours of overtime he puts in when systems his company installs malfunction. He does try to come home on weekends when he travels, but this causes some difficulties with clients who expect him to socialize with them over the weekends and with his bosses who question the extra airplane travel. Toni understands Carl's traveling, but also resents the additional work and parenting which falls on her shoulders when Carl is gone week after week. Toni would like to return to college to pick up some courses that would enable her to expand her teaching credentials, but feels she cannot until Carl stops most of his business trips.

Toni is active in a tennis league and would like to advance in competition with her friends, but is worried about doing so because the next level of competition would involve occasional weekends away from home. She feels torn between the need to be with friends who share her love of tennis and leaving her children and husband. Carl plays racquetball with a childhood friend every Saturday when he's in town and coaches the seven-years-old's soccer team in the fall. He is involved with a fund-raising committee at church and has meetings with other soccer coaches to review coaching strategies. Carl and Toni argue about their schedules, the children's needs, and their career demands, yet they see their friends dealing with the same issues in their marriages.

1.   List the ascribed and achieved statuses for Carl and Toni.

| **Carl** | | **Toni** | |
| *ascribed* | *achieved* | *ascribed* | *achieved* |

2.   What roles do Carl and Toni play?

Carl   **Toni**

3.   Which statuses would you identify as master status(es) for Carl? For Toni?

Carl   **Toni**

4.   What is Carl's status set? Toni's?

Carl   **Toni**

5.   What role conflict and/or role strain do you see Carl and Toni experiencing? Describe it.

6.   Identify a primary group for Carl and Toni. Secondary group(s).

7.   What is an in-group for Carl? For Toni? Identify a reference group.

<u>**Carl**</u>   <u>**Toni**</u>

in-group:

reference group:

EXERCISE #3

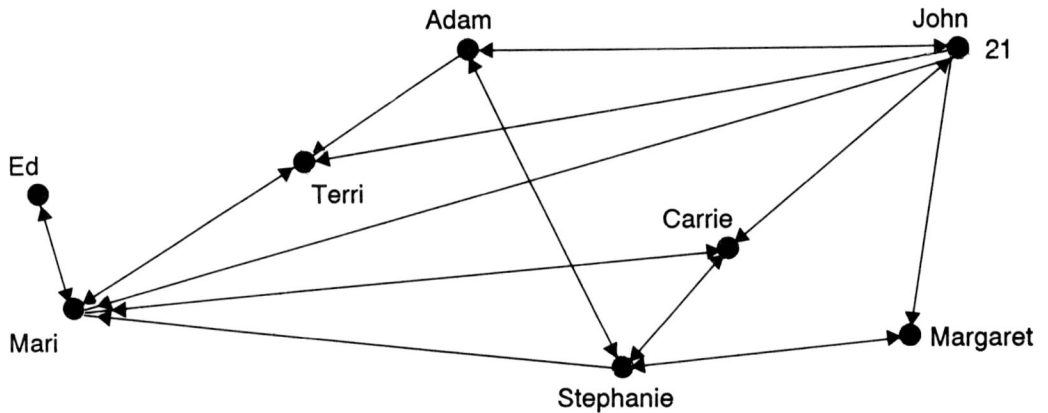

1.   Looking at this sociogram, who would you say is most isolated? Who is least isolated?

   a.   most isolated:

   b.   least isolated:

2.   Ask a group of people at work or a group of your mutual friends to answer these questions:

  a.   With whom would you like to eat lunch?

  b.   With whom would you like to sit next to at a concert?

  c.   With whom would you like to be next door neighbors?

  d.   With whom would you like to spend most of your free time?

3.   Construct a sociogram and describe the relationships you learned about in the previous question.

EXERCISE #4

Describe a work experience in your life in which you can detail how you exhibited frontstage and backstage behavior.

1.   *Frontstage*

2.   *Backstage*

3.   What was the definition of the situation in each instance?

Frontstage

Backstage

CHAPTER 4
The Social Self

LEARNING OBJECTIVES

After reading Chapter 4, you should be able to:

1. Explain the nature of the socialization process and how we become socialized.

2. Discuss the effects of early, extreme isolation on human beings and its impact on the socialization process.

3. Evaluate the role evolution has played in shaping human beings as social creatures.

4. Outline the elements involved in describing how people learn appropriate role behavior through information, rehearsal, feedback, and social supports.

5. Examine subcultural differences in socializing children, especially that of parental occupation.

6. Compare and contrast the traditional and modern patterns of child-rearing.

7. Summarize the effects the agents of socialization have on children as they grow up.

8. Explain the views of Charles Horton Cooley, George Herbert Mead, and Erving Goffman in the formation of the self.

9. Discuss other views in the development of self-concept and what factors have not been traditionally integrated into the study of personality by sociologists.

10. Present the stages of psychosexual development proposed by Freud and explain his views on the conflict between self and society, the unconscious, and the construction of the self as a psychosocial process.

11. Outline the stages of cognitive development presented by Erik Erikson and his views on the linkage between this essentially psychological perspective and sociology.

12. Note how Piaget's theory of cognitive development ties into Mead's ideas about the development of role-taking.

13. Explain the concepts of cognitive and moral development and illustrate using Kohlberg and Gilligan's perspectives.

14. Explain B.F. Skinner's notions of the Skinner box, the perspective of behaviorism, and how it may be applied.

15. Review the ideas on how personalities are shaped cross-culturally.

GLOSSARY CONCEPTS

socialization (p. 96)
validation of self (p. 98)
anticipatory socialization (p. 99)
modeling (p. 100)
positive sanctions (p. 100)
negative sanctions (p. 100)
agents of socialization (p. 103)
reciprocal socialization (p. 104)
peers (p. 104)
mentors (p. 106)
self-identity (p. 107)
looking-glass self (p. 107)
gesture (p. 108)
significant others (p. 108)
generalized others (p. 108)
play (p. 109)
games (p. 109)

"I" (p. 109)
"me" (p. 109)
virtual self (p. 110)
role distance (p. 110)
deindividualization (p. 110)
affective factor (p. 112)
cognitive factors (p. 112)
repression (p. 112)
ego defenses (p. 113)
ego development (p. 113)
ego identity (p. 115)
cognitive development (p. 112)
moral reasoning (p. 115)
behaviorism (p. 118)
Skinner box (p. 119)
desocialization (p. 120)
resocialization (p. 120)

REVEIW QUESTIONS

Fill-In Questions

Fill in the blanks in the sentences below with the correct word or items.

1. The process of _____ involves learning how to behave in society, the transmission of culture, and the development of the self. (p. 96)

2. Human infants are born a bundle of potentials and are helpless in terms of _____ dependency. (p. 98)

3. Physical dependence on other people is an essential precondition to _____. (p. 98)

4. The responses from others which are essential across a person's life span are: validation of self, affection, nurturance for physical survival, and _____. (p. 98)

5. The elements involved in role learning are: rehearsal, feedback from role partners, _____ _____ and information. (p. 99, 100)

6. The most crucial of all subcultural differences observed in the socialization of children is _____ _____. (p. 100)

7. Parents in white-collar occupations encourage their children to _____, while blue-collar parents tend to emphasize conformity. (p. 101)

8. The first and most important agents of socialization are the _____. (p. 103)

9. Culture is _____ in a child's mind through parental expectations. (p. 103)

10. George Herbert Mead's concept of the _____ other refers to widely held standards of acceptable behavior for anyone in a given status. (p. 108)

11. Imitation, play, and _____ are the three stages Mead argued that are essential to role taking. (p. 109)

12. The _____ is the spontaneous and creative element of the self, while the _____ consists of the internalized attitudes of others. (p. 109)

13. A(n) _____ _____, or possible self, awaits us in each role we perform. (p. 110)

14. Two major aspects of personality development are the _____, which has to do with feelings, and the _____ which has to do with how people think and process information. (p. 112)

15. Freud argued that civilization, or society, is based on the control of _____. (p. 112)

16. Erikson proposed that the life course is composed of a series of _____ that require reorganization of the ego. (p. 113)

17. Kohlberg's notions of moral development are based on data from _____. (p. 118)

18. Skinner claims that all behavior is shaped by the _____ of rewards. (p. 118)

19. _____ involves learning to give up a role and _____ involves learning radically new norms and values. (p. 120)

True-False Questions

*Circle **T** if the statement is true. Circle **F** if the statement is false.*

T F 1. Humans become human beings through interaction with others. (p. 96)

T F 2. Extreme isolation causes problems for children but not for adults. (p. 97)

T F 3. Maternal or mothering instincts can be observed among some primitive humans. (p. 97)

T F 4. Interaction with other humans is essential to remain a healthy, stable person. (p. 98)

T F 5. Genetic tendencies produce behavior almost automatically. (p. 98)

T F 6. Parents in highly supervised work tend toward a "psychological" approach in disciplining their children. (p. 101)

T F 7. During the teen years, peers have more influence on immediate lifestyle choices, while parents have more influence on basic values. (p. 105)

T F 8. The self is rooted in social interaction. (p. 107)

T F 9. Play is disorganized, spontaneous and may involve an imaginary playmate. (p. 109)

T F 10. According to Mead, there is no necessary conflict between the "I" and the "me" because both are needed to form the self. (p. 110)

T F 11. Role distance protects the self and offers some freedom of personal style. (p. 110)

T F 12. Freud argued that social life is impossible unless people can control their behavior. (p. 112)

T F 13. Blaming others, repression, and denial are all examples of ego defenses. (p. 113)

T F 14. Erikson extended the stages of personality growth and change to cover the time period from early adolescence to middle-age. (p. 113)

T F 15. The moral development stages proposed by Kohlberg have been criticized because the highest good is described in terms of the work ethic. (p. 118)

T F 16. Girls, but not women, bring a different set of values to their moral judgments than do boys. (p. 118)

T F 17. Behaviorists focus on observable and measurable actions. (p. 118)

T F 18. Different socialization practices and experiences produce different types of people. (p. 120)

T F 19. The transitions of middle and late life can best be viewed as "crises." (pp. 116, 117)

Matching Questions

Match items in Column B with the correct answer in Column A (columns continue on next page).

COLUMN A	COLUMN B
1. significant others (p. 108)	a. Involves the application of standards of right and wrong.
2. self identity (p. 107)	b. The placing of unpleasant and unacceptable emotions below the level of consciousness.
3. gesture (p. 108)	
4. psychoanalysis (p. 110)	c. Involves rehearsing prior to assuming a role.
5. role distance (p. 110)	d. The space placed by a person between the self and the self-in-the-role.
6. agents of socialization (p. 103)	e. The link between culture and social structure; a dual process.
7. ego defenses (p. 113)	f. Copying of characteristics of admired persons.
8. looking-glass self (p. 107)	g. A symbol shared by group members.
	h. Children modifying their parents' view of the world.
9. validation of self (p. 99)	i. More organized than play and often competitive with rules and structure.
10. deindividualization (p. 110)	j. Protective mechanisms developed when we fear losing control.

11. mentors (p. 106)

12. modeling (p. 100)

13. ego identity (p. 115)

14. repression (p. 112)

15. reciprocal socialization (p. 104)

16. socialization (p. 96)

17. anticipatory socialization (p. 99)

18. games (p. 109)

19. moral reasoning (p. 115)

k. Persons whose affection and approval are particularly desired.

l. Requires that one is who one claims to be.

m. People and organizations responsible for teaching rules and roles.

n. An organization of perceptions about who and what kind of person one is.

o. Depersonalization; a process of removing a person's civilian identity.

p. Suggests that we see ourselves reflected back in the reactions of other.

q. Teachers who act as guides and sponsors.

r. A sense of continuity and sameness in the self across time and in different situations.

s. Founded by Freud and involves both the study of the unconscious motivations and the treatment of the symptoms of emotional distress.

ANSWERS
Answers to Fill-In Questions

1. socialization
2. physical
3. learning
4. approval
5. social supports
6. parental occupation
7. question
8. parents
9. internalized
10. generalized
11. game
12. "I"; "me"
13. virtual self
14. affective; cognitive
15. impulse
16. challenges
17. males or men
18. manipulation
19. desocialization; resocialization

Answers to True-False Questions

1. T
2. F
3. F
4. T
5. F
6. F
7. T
8. T
9. F
10. T
11. T
12. T
13. T
14. F
15. T
16. F
17. T
18. T
19. F

Answers to Matching Questions

1. k
2. n
3. g
4. s
5. d
6. m
7. j
8. p
9. l
10. o
11. q
12. f
13. r
14. b
15. h
16. e
17. c
18. i
19. a

EXERCISE #1

Daniel is eight-years old and attends a private school which has small classes. Daniel and his friends at school collect colorful stickers. Those who have large, impressive sticker collections have a higher status than those whose collections are small and unimpressive. Daniel wants to enjoy the flattery of his friends and wants to feel important by having the largest, most "awesome" sticker collection in his class. When he spots a particularly desirable sticker in Harris' desk, he impulsively takes it. Harris immediately notices the loss of his important sticker and complains to the teacher who confronts Daniel. At first Daniel denies responsibility, but when the stolen sticker turns up in his spelling book, he admits his guilt. The teacher calls Daniel's parents and reports the incident.

1.   You are Daniel's parent. You are in a white-collar occupation. How will you handle this situation?

   a.   What are the consequences of your actions for Daniel?

2.   As Daniel's parent, you have to handle the situation but now you hold a blue-collar job. What will you do?

   a.   What will the consequences of your actions for Daniel?

EXERCISE #2

Specifically describe how each of the following agents of socialization has shaped your life. Provide two examples for each by relating incidents that have been significant for you.

1. Parents

    1.

    2.

2. Peers

    1.

    2.

3. Teachers

    1.

    2.

4. Media

    1.

    2.

CHAPTER 5
Deviance and Crime

LEARNING OBJECTIVES

After reading Chapter 5, you should be able to:

1. Explain the nature of deviant behavior, how sociologists view and define deviancy and conformity.

2. Evaluate how conformity is structured, why conformity to some norms is more important than conformity to others, and how expectations for behavior change over time.

3. Outline the social functions of deviance.

4. Explore the dimensions of who benefits from retaining prostitution as a safety valve or an expression of discontent.

5. Define social control, and explain its significance for conformity and deviance.

6. Summarize the biological, psychological and sociological explanations of deviance.

7. Compare the structural and process theories which explain deviancy.

8. Explain the nature of deviant vs. nondeviant careers.

9. Explain the difference between the deviant, the eccentric and relate these ideas to petty and institutionalized evasions of norms.

10. Review the explanations and research that emphasize social reasons, problems, and stereotypes for mental illness.

11. Differentiate criminal from civil law.

12. Discuss the three ideas which explain how norms become laws: social injury, consensus, and conflict.

13. Explain the most feared of all crimes: street crime and then review the two methods by which is reported in the U.S., including the shortcomings of each reporting method.

14. Explain the nature of such crimes as homicide and property crimes.

15. Define organized or syndicated crime and explain how and why succeeding immigrant groups became involved.

16. Explore the differences between white-collar and organizational crime.

17. Define the nature and scope of crimes without victims, including gambling and drug use.

18. Define who juveniles are and the differences such definitions may make for juvenile lawbreakers.

19. Examine the unique role and duties of the police.

20. Summarize the roles of the players in the adult judicial system.

21. Trace the steps of the accused through the judicial system including prison.

22. Discuss how different philosophies have shaped our views of capital punishment and incarceration.

23. Explain why prisons are considered total institutions and then describe today's prison conditions.

GLOSSARY CONCEPTS

deviant behavior (p. 125)
proscriptive norms (p. 128)
prescriptive norms (p. 128)
boundary setting (p. 131)
confrontations (p. 131)
safety valve (p. 132)
principled challenges (p. 134)
social controls (p. 135)
formal agents of social control (p. 135)
repressive control systems (p. 135)
restrained control systems (p.135)
delinquent and criminal subcultures (p. 139)

labeling theory (p. 140)
differential association (p. 141)
social learning theory (p. 141)
primary deviance (p. 141)
secondary deviance (p. 141)
stigma (p. 142)
deviant subcultures (p. 142)
eccentric behavior (p,. 142)
petty violations of norms (p. 143)
institutionalized evasion of norms (p. 143)
residual deviance (p. 143)
career contingencies (p. 144)

circuit of agents (p. 144)
deinstitutionalization (p. 145)
criminal law (p. 147)
civil law (p. 147)
social injury model (p. 148)
consensus model (p. 148)
conflict model (p. 148)
culture conflict model (p. 148)
street crimes (p. 149)
Uniform Crime Reports (p.149)
index crimes (p. 150)
National Crime Survey (p.150)
property crimes (p. 151)
organized crime (p. 153)
white collar crimes (p. 154)

organizational (p.154)
crimes without victims (p. 157)
juveniles (p. 158)
status offense (p. 158)
juvenile court system (p. 161)
police (p. 161)
prosecutor (p. 163)
defense attorney (p. 163)
judge (p. 163)
plea bargaining (p. 163)
capital punishment (p. 164)
rehabilitation (p. 166)
total institutions (p. 166)
predispositional (p.167
situational view (p. 167)

REVIEW QUESTIONS
Fill-In Questions

Fill in the blanks in the sentences with the correct word or items.

1. Sociologists primarily are concerned with _____ _____ deviation from social norms when discussing deviant behavior. (p. 125)

2. What is defined as deviance _____ over time. (p. 129)

3. In Durkheim's view, crime and other forms of deviance fulfill an important service by generating social _____. (p. 131)

4. Expressions of approval, like smiles, receiving gifts, or hugs are examples of _____ _____ of social control. (p. 135)

5. A(n) _____ control system makes use of extensive power to ensure people conform. (p. 135)

6. Sheldon, who classified people according to _____ _____, stated that endomorphs tend toward manic depression and alcoholism. (p. 136)

7. _____ theories have in common that deviancy is the result of moral or mental flaws within the individual. (p. 137)

8. _____ theories of deviancy are concerned with why deviance exists in every known society, how people become deviant, and what mechanisms for social control are used. (p. 137)

9. _____ theories of deviance, which are macro-level, emphasize explanations of the differences in type and amount of deviant behavior among people occupying various statuses, while _____ theories, which are micro-level, focus on how individuals are socialized into deviant behaviors. (p. 138)

10. When a society's resources for controlling deviance are overwhelmed by too many violators, _____ _____ is likely to occur. (p. 138)

11. Merton argued that the _____ is resigned to fate and tends to over conform to the rules of good conduct. (pp. 138, 139)

12. Criminal, conflict-oriented, and retreatist subcultures may arise from _____ _____ _____. (p. 139)

13. _____ _____ theory maintains that for punishment to be effective, it must take place near the time the deviance occurred. (p. 141)

14. _____ deviance goes undetected or excused by others but _____ deviance results from the social responses which people make to problems created by the social response to deviance. (p. 141)

15. The last step in a deviant career involves a supportive network called a(n) _____ _____. (p. 142)

16. _____ _____ of norms can occur within an organization and norms may be ignored for organizational gain. (p. 143)

17. It is only when behaviors become _____ or _____ to others that a person is most likely to be labeled mentally ill. (p. 144)

18. A _____ _____ _____ is needed to define someone as a mental patient. (p. 144)

19. _____ is the release of mental patients into the community. (p. 145)

20. When sanctions are applied to everyone who commits a certain act, we call this the rule of _____. (p. 148)

21. The _____ model is based on the notion that norms become laws because they reflect customs and general agreement about appropriate behavior. (p. 148)

22. The _____ _____ model emphasizes value differences. (p. 148)

23. _____ crimes are actions that directly threatens persons or property. (p. 149)

24. African-American men between the ages of 20 and 24 are at the area at risk for _____ crime. (p. 149)

25. Index crimes most often are committed by the _____ and _____. (p. 150)

26. The Justice Department conducts a(n) _____ _____ _____ twice a year and gathers data on victimization. (p. 150)

27. A(n) _____ _____ _____ may exist which has physical aggression as the norm. (p. 151)

28. Crime, including white collar crime, is caused by three necessary conditions: neutralization of social controls _____ and _____. (p. 154)

29. The _____ does not raise new revenue and bettors are victimized by poor odds. (p. 158)

30. Violation of a curfew law, being truant from school, running away from home, or being incorrigible are examples of _____ _____. (p. 158)

31. Below the age of _____ a child is considered by the courts as incapable of committing a crime. (p. 159)

32. The three principal participants in the judicial process are the judge, _____, and defense attorney. (p. 163)

33. The single most important factor in determining the size of a prison population is the number of _____ _____. (p. 164)

34. The two countries in the world which approve capital punishment are the United States and _____ _____. (p. 165)

35. The history of prisons is based on two opposing philosophies which come from our Protestant value system: _____ and _____. (p. 166)

36. The _____ view assumes that there is a tendency among certain people to act in certain ways but the _____ view assumes that the social situation, statuses, and roles assigned to people produce certain types of behavior. (p. 167)

37.   Most of the inmates in a(n) _____ have not yet been convicted of any crime. (p. 167)

True-False Questions

*Circle **T** if the statement is true. Circle **F** if the statement is false.*

T   F   1.   The principle concern of sociologists who study deviant behavior is to discover why people do not conform to rules. (p. 125)

T   F   2.   The relative power of competing groups determines which standards of right and wrong become the norm for the group. (pp. 125, 126)

T   F   3.   Since there is no one universal standard of behavior, all norms are arbitrary. (p. 129)

T   F   4.   What is defined as deviant depends on the social and political context. (p. 134)

T   F   5.   Biological theories of deviancy all have in common the idea that there is something basically wrong with the deviant. (p. 136)

T   F   6.   Behavior we often label deviant reflects the cultural values of the society in which it occurs. (p. 138)

T   F   7.   The chronic drug addict would be described by Merton as a rebel. (p. 139)

T   F   8.   The idea that deviance is created in the process of interaction is basic to conflict theory. (p. 139)

T   F   9.   Labels can create and maintain deviant behavior. (p. 140)

T   F   10.   Differential association theory states that people become deviant because of certain unfortunate experiences or personal traits. (p. 141)

T   F   11.   Eccentrics, like deviants, are recognized rule breakers. (p. 142)

T   F   12.   Diagnosis of mental illnesses tend to reflect the norms of the times. (p. 143)

T   F   13.   Career contingencies may involve the occupation and income of the rule breaker, and the types of norms broken. (p. 144)

T   F   14.   Conduct directed against private persons is considered to be criminal law. (p. 147)

T   F   15.   Control of crime is a profitable financial investment. (p. 148)

T   F   16.   Most violent crimes involve people of the same race and are committed during daylight hours. (p. 149)

T   F   17.   Nonviolent and serious violent crimes are included in the *Uniform Crime Reports*. (p. 150)

T F 18. Most crimes are not reported. (p. 151)

T F 19. People in rural areas are more likely to report property crime than are urban dwellers. (p. 151)

T F 20. Women's crimes tend to be linked to their gender role. (p. 153)

T F 21. Organized crime is a Sicilian phenomenon in the United States of this century. (p. 154)

T F 22. The cost of corporate crime is greater than the cost of auto theft, larceny, robbery, and burglary. (p. 155)

T F 23. Police are formal agents of social control. (p. 161)

T F 24. Today, most cases in the legal system are settled by jury trial. (p. 163)

T F 25. The chances of avoiding arrest and conviction are high in the United States. (p. 164)

T F 26. Rehabilitate means to return to a previous state based on repentance and salvation. (p. 166)

T F 27. As reflected in our penal system, it is possible to rehabilitate and punish at the same time. (p. 166)

T F 28. Prison norms are *inconsistent* with rehabilitation. (p. 167)

Matching Questions

Match items in Column B with the correct answer in Column A (columns continue on next page).

COLUMN A	COLUMN B
1. labeling theory (p. 140)	a. Mental illness.
	b. These may be tolerated because their position, wealth, or knowledge protect them.
2. boundary setting (p. 131)	
	c. These test the limits of acceptable behavior.
3. differential association (p. 141)	
	d. These develop primarily among poorer juveniles who are relatively unskilled at competing in a middle-class world.
4. residual deviance (p. 142)	
5. prescriptive norms (p. 128)	e. A way of releasing frustration, tension, or anger.
6. stigma (p. 142)	f. Focuses on the formation and application of social definitions and on the process of defining behavior as deviant.
7. safety valve (p. 132)	

COLUMN A

8.   eccentrics (p. 142)

9.   Durkheim's idea of deviance (p. 131)

10.   restrained systems of social control (p. 135)

11.   social control (p. 135)

12.   delinquent subcultures (p. 139)

13.   confrontations (p. 131)

14.   property crimes (p. 151)

15.   juvenile court system (p. 161)

16.   index crimes (p. 150)

17.   white collar crimes (p. 154)

18.   police (p. 161)

19.   organizational crimes (p. 154)

20.   juveniles (p. 158)

21.   organized crime (p. 153)

22.   total institutions (p. 166)

23.   recidivist (p. 167)

COLUMN B

g.   A morally undesirable label that tends to be generalized to other undesirable characteristics as well.

h.   These are characterized by limits on the invasion of personal privacy and tolerance of variation in conformity to norms; example would be the U.S.

i.   Occurs when shared norms and values set the limits of acceptable behavior.

j.   Deviance is necessary to societal well-being.

k.   Criminal behavior is learned within primary groups.

l.   These dictate what is expected; "thou shalt."

m.   Techniques for getting people to obey norms.

n.   Illegal activities committed by persons of high status, usually nonviolent, for their own benefit.

o.   They have the right to use coercive force to control behavior.

p.   Continued organized endeavors to accumulate wealth in defiance of the law.

q.   Burglaries, theft, and larceny.

r.   Crimes carried out in one's role as employee to achieve corporate goals.

s.   Murder, robbery, aggravated assault, and forcible rape.

t.   They come to the attention of the law because they have committed a status offense, a crime, or have been neglected or abused.

u.   The court system designed to protect children and adolescents from the stresses of labeling and severe punishments.

v.   Repeat offender.

w.   Prisons and jails.

ANSWERS

Answers to Fill-In Questions

1. socially disapproved
2. changes
3. cohesion
4. informal mechanisms
5. repressive
6. body types
7. psychological
8. sociological
9. structural; process
10. social change
11. ritualist
12. blocked opportunity structure
13. social learning
14. primary; secondary
15. deviant subculture
16. institutionalized evasion
17. disruptive; threatening
18. circuit of agents
19. deinstitutionalization
20. law
21. consensus
22. culture conflict
23. street
24. violent
25. poor; powerless
26. *National Crime Survey*
27. subculture of violence
28. motivation, neutralization of social controls, opportunity
29. lottery
30. status offenses
31. seven
32. prosecutor
33. cells available
34. South Africa
35. rehabilitation; punishment
36. predispositional; situational
37. jail

Answers to True-False Questions

1. F
2. T
3. T
4. T
5. T
6. T
7. F
8. F
9. T
10. F
11. T
12. T
13. T
14. F
15. T
16. T
17. F
18. T
19. F
20. T
21. F
22. T
23. T
24. F
25. T
26. T
27. F
28. T

Answers to Matching Questions

1. f
2. i
3. k
4. a
5. l
6. g
7. e
8. b
9. j
10. h
11. m
12. d
13. c
14. q
15. u
16. s
17. n
18. o
19. r
20. t
21. p
22. w
23. v

EXERCISE #1

The authors of your text raise some questions about deviancy which you can consider by reflecting on the society in which we live.

1. What *categories* of people in this society do you think we widely regard as being deviant? Explain why you believe each category is worthy of being "deviant." Remember that these categories of people must be perceived as threatening to the norms and values of our society.

Category   **Explanation**

2. Examine your listing of categories of people. Which categories of deviance do you believe the people in power in this society share with you?

EXERCISE #2

Newspapers and news magazines constantly run stories about all types of deviancy, including criminal activities, cheating, violence, etc. Find four articles reflecting four different kinds of deviance from your local newspaper or from news magazines and answer the following questions.

1. Using Merton's typology on pages 138 and 139, illustrate the different kinds of deviance you found in terms of the goals and means.

Kind of Deviance	Goals	Means
A.		
B.		
C.		
D.		

2. Considering the theories presented in the Chapter, which one(s) do you think best explain why each type of deviancy discussed in each of your four articles occurred.

Theory	*Why* you think this is the best theory
A.	
B.	
C.	
D.	

EXERCISE #3

In the newspaper or in a news magazine, locate an article on each *type* of crime discussed in the chapter. Attach your articles to this exercise.

1. For each type of crime, find a theory from the chapter on deviancy, or from this chapter which you believe best explains why the crime was committed. Explain why you feel the theory you choose is the best to explain the crime.

    Type of Crime   **Theory**   **Why this theory is the best explanation**

EXERCISE #4

Boise, Idaho has the lowest homicide rate in the United States. In fact, there has not been a homicide in Boise since December 10, 1988. Boise is a city of 120,000 people and there have been only seven murders in the last four and a half years. No police officer has even been killed on the job. The national murder rate in 1988 was 8.4 murders per 100,000 people. Boise does have other crime problems, though, but robbery is not one of them. Boise ranks last in robberies and is in the bottom quarter of the FBI's violent crime category. The city has grown twenty-five percent in the last ten years. It has one major east-west highway in and out of the city. The population in the county is 91.9 percent white, 0.6 percent African-American, 3.7 percent Latino, and 3.8 percent other minorities. Boise ranks sixth in the nation in the number of major corporate headquarters per capita. Hewlett-Packard Co. is the largest employer in the area.

1.   Explain why a city of Boise's size is free of homicide.

2.   Using information from your text, and the information above, speculate as to why Boise would have such a low robbery rate.

CHAPTER 6
Social Stratification

LEARNING OBJECTIVES

After reading Chapter 6, you should be able to:

1. Understand the three kinds of valued resources found in all societies and how social hierarchies are formed.

2. Discuss the principal features of the functional and conflict theories of social stratification and then discuss a unified view of these explanations.

3. Distinguish the dimensions of social stratification: power, prestige, and property.

4. Explain why the middle class is shrinking.

5. Discuss the importance of SES as the key indicator of social position.

6. Compare and contrast class awareness, class consciousness and self-perception.

7. List the ideological justifications for the American social class system and explain how they are related to social order.

8. Define the various ways poverty may be explained and identify who the poor really are in the United States and how they have been helped.

9. Identify the very wealthy who are at the top of the social class system and describe their lifestyle.

10.   Discuss social mobility in class and caste systems, and then examine types of mobility, including: intergenerational and intragenerational mobility in the United States, structural or demand mobility, and relative mobility vs. absolute mobility.

11.   Explain how status cues, symbols, consistencies and inconsistencies affect life on a day-to-day basis.

GLOSSARY CONCEPTS

stratification (p. 175)
power (p. 175)
property (p. 175)
social hierarchy (p. 175)
meritocracy (p. 175)
social stratification (p. 177)
authority (p. 178)
influence (p. 178)
network (p. 179)
socioeconomic status (SES) (p. 184)
class awareness (p. 184)
class consciousness (p. 186)
poverty level (p. 191)
feminization of poverty (p. 193)

workfare (p. 190)
social mobility (p. 196)
caste systems (p. 197)
apartheid (p. 197)
intergenerational (p. 198)
intragenerational (p. 198)
structural or demand (p. 198)
class immobility (p. 201)
deferred gratification (p. 201)
status attainment (p. 202)
status symbols (p. 203)
status consistency (p. 204)
status inconsistency (p. 204)

REVIEW QUESTIONS
Fill-In Questions

Fill in the blanks in the sentences below with the correct word or items.

1.   A set of ranked statuses from highest to lowest is a social _____ which tends to be diamond shaped. (p. 175)

2.   Once a society's economy produces a division of labor beyond gathering, people who do different types of work are _____ rewarded. (p. 175)

3. In contrast to functional explanations of inequality, conflict explanations focus on _____ variables rather than personal ones. (p. 177)

4. Social stratification refers to hierarchies of statuses in a society that reflect the _____ distribution of power, prestige, and property. (p. 177)

5. Power that belongs to a socially recognized status is known as _____. while _____ is the ability to persuade others to follow one's will. (p. 178)

6. _____ _____ consists of the value of all assets minus all debts. (p. 179)

7. Asset ownership varies the most by _____. (p. 179)

8. _____ _____ comes from wages, salaries, dividends, and capital gains which people report to the IRS. (p. 181)

9. The increase of part-time employees who do not receive fringe benefits is a reason that the _____ _____ is disappearing. (p. 184)

10. _____ _____ is a measure of social class based on a combination of income, occupational prestige and education. (p. 184)

11. _____ is the most powerful variable in the social sciences. (p. 184)

12. Social order is threatened when _____ is defined as unfair. (p. 186)

13. Most Americans explain poverty in terms of the characteristics of the _____. (p. 187)

14. Americans accept inequalities as legitimate when they can attribute success or failure to _____. (p. 189)

15. For white women, poverty is often the result of _____. (p. 193)

16. The cause of inner-city poverty is _____. (p. 194)

17. The upper class maintains its continuity over time through _____ and the socialization of its children in a series of private schools. (p. 196)

18. _____ systems are based on ascribed statuses, with minimal movement across stratum boundaries. (p. 197)

19. _____ mobility is perceived as a disgrace to family and a denial of the meaning of our society. (p. 198)

20. The structure of the _____ determines mobility rates. (p. 198)

21. It is likely that upward mobility rates will be relatively _____ for people born between 1967 and 1972. (p. 201)

22. Class _____ occurs when social rank is reproduced from one generation to another. (p. 201)

23. Status _____ are the outward signs of social rank. (p. 203)

24. Status _____ occurs when a person occupies a similar rank across different hierarchies, but an African-American physician would present a case of status _____. (p. 204)

True-False Questions

*Circle **T** if the statement is true. Circle **F** if the statement is false.*

T   F   1.   A basic assumption of the functional perspective is that some forms of inequality are inevitable and beneficial. (p. 176)

T   F   2.   Sociologists have long held the opinion that the functionalist explanation of stratification most clearly and accurately explains inequality. (pp.176, 177)

T   F   3.   The functional and conflict explanations of inequality are mutually exclusive. (p. 177)

T   F   4.   The actual distribution of property in the United States is difficult to trace. (p. 180)

T   F   5.   Younger singles have more assets than married people over the age of fifty-five. (p. 181)

T   F   6.   Households tend to have *lower* incomes than do families. (p. 182)

T   F   7.   The middle class has been slowly increasing since the mid-1960s. (p. 182)

T   F   8.   All methods of measuring social class focus on the individual. (p. 184)

T   F   9.   Americans see themselves as having a class free society and so do not see class differences. (p. 185)

T   F   10.   There has been no class struggle in the United States because labor has been dominated by government and business. (p. 186)

T   F   11.   Inequality produces social disorder in nearly every case known. (p. 186)

T   F   12.   The cultural promise of equal opportunity is a myth. (p. 187)

T   F   13.   Individual traits are responsible for success or failure in the workplace. (p. 189)

T   F   14.   The poor are poor because they compete for jobs in sectors of the economy that offer little security and pay low wages. (p. 189)

T   F   15.   The 1960s "War on Poverty" lowered poverty rates, primarily because the elderly, unemployed fathers and Appalachian whites were helped. (pp. 190, 191)

T   F   16.   There is evidence that indicates women would rather stay home with their children and be on welfare than work. (p. 193)

T   F   17.   Being wealthy automatically puts you in the upper class. (p. 196)

T   F   18.   The United States currently has elements of a caste system. (p. 198)

T   F   19.   Occupational shifts, free education and low birth rates among the middle class account for the spurt in upward mobility between 1945 and 1965. (p. 198)

T   F   20.   Being successful in this country is influenced greatly by the social status of the family into which one is born. (p. 201)

T   F   21.   In the status attainment model, family background plays a key role. (p. 202)

Matching Questions

Match items in Column B with the correct answer in Column A (columns continue on next page).

COLUMN A	COLUMN B
1. SSI (p. 190)	a. Max Weber's three separate dimensions.
	b. Children and their mothers.
2. kinds of valued resources (p. 175)	c. The control of cultural symbols.
	d. Movement of people and groups within the stratification system.
3. poverty level (p. 191)	
	e. A hierarchy based on ability and credentials.
4. deferred gratification (p. 201)	
	f. Societal-level factors affecting mobility rates.
5. intergenerational mobility (p. 198)	
	g. Power, prestige, and property.
6. power (p. 175)	h. Status changes between parents and their adult children.
7. social mobility (p. 196)	i. Refers to the amount of money received in a given year as reported by households, families, and individuals.
8. class awareness (p. 184)	
	j. Recognition of differences in income, occupational prestige, and social power.
9. class consciousness (p. 186)	
	k. Represents the minimum income required to stay alive.
10. class, status group, and parties (p. 178)	

COLUMN A	COLUMN B
11. most welfare recipients (p. 192)	l. Occurs when class awareness becomes the central organizing point of self-definition and political actions.
12. meritocracy (p. 176)	m. Postponing of current pleasure to achieve future goals.
13. structural or demand mobility (p. 198)	n. Covers aid to the blind, disabled, and the elderly at about half the poverty level.
14. ideological hegemony (p. 176)	o. The ability to impose your will on another.
15. earned income (p. 181)	

ANSWERS

Answers to Fill-In Questions

1. hierarchy
2. differentially or unequally
3. structural
4. unequal
5. authority; influence
6. net worth
7. race
8. earned income
9. middle class
10. socioeconomic status
11. class
12. inequality
13. poor
14. themselves
15. divorce
16. joblessness
17. intermarriage
18. caste
19. downward
20. economy
21. low
22. immobility
23. symbols
24. consistency; inconsistency

Answers to True-False Questions

1. T
2. F
3. F
4. T
5. F
6. T
7. F
8. T
9. F
10. T
11. F
12. T
13. F
14. T
15. T
16. F
17. F
18. T
19. T
20. T
21. T

Answers to Matching Questions

1. n
2. g
3. k
4. m
5. h
6. o
7. d
8. j
9. l
10. a
11. b
12. e
13. f
14. c
15. i

EXERCISE #1

We have all been exposed to media stories about political efforts to help reduce the welfare roles. Many of these efforts are directed toward women who have dependent children. A program in Michigan called, Living in Family Environments, (L.I.F.E.), seeks to match welfare recipients and severely disabled children. The adults become foster parents to the children and go off welfare. The state pays the adult to take care of the child and pays medical care for the child. Benefits to the state include the costs saved by having the adult off the welfare roles, and costs saved by having the disabled child out of an institution. Foster parents are given seven days of orientation and twenty hours of training in a foster home. Some other states are looking into similar programs.

1.   List at least three benefits to a welfare recipient who becomes a foster parent to a severely disabled child.

   A.

   B.

   C.

2.   List three benefits to a severely disabled child who is matched with a foster parent.

   A.

   B.

   C.

EXERCISE #2

Kari and Walter both work and have college educations. Kari makes $34,000 per year as an advertising executive, and Walter earns $63,000 in a managerial position for a large corporation. They have two children who attend the local public school. Three years ago Kari looked at her home and became dissatisfied with it. She convinced her husband that a large edition to their family room, a sky light, french doors, and an expanded kitchen would begin to make her more content with her home. After successfully negotiating the loan for her home improvements, Kari realized that their family van was on its last legs. She and Walter spotted a larger van trimmed in cherry wood, with a VCR, TV, and twin stereo systems. Kari and Walter reasoned that the VCR and TV would keep their very active children occupied during the long drives they make several time a year to family members, so they bought the $24,000 van and obtained a home equity loan.

A year and a half ago, Kari looked around her home and let Walter know that the carpeting needed to be replaced as did their living room furniture. Kari explained to Walter that the new carpeting and furniture would help make her content with her home. Six months ago Kari realized what would *really* make her content was a new house. She began house hunting with a realtor and located two houses to show Walter. At first Walter was reluctant to agree to a much larger mortgage but Kari convinced him they could swing the extra money. The kids helped to pressure their father with their excitement about an in-ground pool and other amenities one of the houses had to offer. When a house was decided upon the family moved. The new house had 1900 square feet of living space more than their old house, more rooms, and a larger yard.

Kari and Walter have stopped putting money into tax sheltered annuities for their retirement and the children's education funds to afford this house. Their new next-door neighbors own a local chain of pharmacies and neighbors down the street are successful professionals.

1. To what social class would you assign this family?

2. What label would Karl Marx use to describe Walter?

3.   What status symbols has the family accumulated?

CHAPTER 7
Sex and Gender

LEARNING OBJECTIVES

After reading Chapter 7, you should be able to:

1. Explain the functional, conflict, and symbolic interactionist perspectives on sexuality.

2. Relate the concept of sexual scripts to the socialization process.

3. Discuss the major norms and behaviors identified today that relate to sexual expression in the United States among adults and teenagers.

4. Examine the relationship between sexuality, reproduction, and the law.

5. Explain the homosexual experience in historical and cross-cultural terms, and trace the organizational development for gay rights.

6. Discuss the sociological explanations for the existence of homosexuality, and determine the prevalence of homosexuality and bisexuality in the United States.

7. Identify the types of sexual violence, explain its prevalence and why this violence is usually directed at women and children.

8. Review current changes in our society inspired by the New Feminist Movement: changes in men's lives, public attitudes on a range of issues, and the development of feminist scholarship.

GLOSSARY CONCEPTS

sexual identity (p. 208)
sexual scripts (p. 209)
extramarital sex (p. 211)
abortion (p. 214)
in vitro (p. 218)
homosexuality (p. 218)
gay (p.218)
berdaches (p. 218)
lesbians (p. 218)
homosexual subcultures (p. 219)
homophobia (p. 219
Gay Rights Movement (p. 219)
"coming out" (p. 219)
bisexuality (p. 222)

domestic partners (p. 223)
sexual violence (p. 223)
date rape (p. 224)
pornography (p. 224)
sexual harassment (p. 226)
gender stratification (p. 227)
male and female (p. 227)
feminine and masculine (p. 227)
patriarchy (p. 230)
cognitive structures (p. 233)
gender inequality (p. 234)
tokenism (p. 236)
gender wage gap (p. 241)
sex segregation (p. 241)

REVIEW QUESTIONS

Fill-In Questions

Fill in the blanks in the sentences below with the correct word or items.

1. _____ _____ refers to seeing yourself as female or male and having the culturally shaped aspects of masculinity or femininity. (p. 208)

2. A task for _____ is to develop a sense of being female or male without linking these identities to sexual meanings. (p. 210)

3. Long-term intimate relationships are increasingly based on _____ factors. (p. 210)

4. From the 1600s to the mid 1800s, sexuality was closely tied to _____. (p. 211)

5. There is a trend toward the _____ of sexuality. (p. 212)

6. Being sexually active for girls is related to low _____ - _____ (p. 213)

7. Public support for sex education in school is due to alarm over the spread of AIDS and
   _____. (pp. 213, 214)

8. _____-_____ teenagers are most at risk for adolescent pregnancies. (p. 215)

9. Teenagers living in the _____ _____ have the
   highest rates of abortions, births, and unintended pregnancies. (p. 215)

10. One argument concerning homosexuality is that it has meaning only in societies where
    maleness and femaleness are assumed to be _____ and opposite
    traits. (p. 218)

11. Some _____ define AIDS as the "gay plague," or God's revenge
    against sexual perversion. (p. 220)

12. Gay men are most tolerated in today's world when they hold _____ jobs.
    (p. 220)

13. Sociologists view homosexual behavior as _____ rather than
    biologically constructed. (p. 221)

14. Recent research on homosexuality focuses on the _____ of an individual's
    experience rather than a single feature. (p. 221)

15. Typically, the relationship between homosexuals are _____. (p. 222)

16. Homosexual parents tend to raise children whose sexual orientation is clearly
    _____ and who are emotionally stable. (p. 223)

17. Sexual violence is directed at the _____, women and children. (p. 223)

18. Private matters, like sexual violence, become public when large numbers of people are
    involved, when incidents are _____, and when the definition of the
    situation changes so the public responds with anger. (p. 223)

19. Feminists see sexual violence as a means of reinforcing male _____.
    (p. 224)

20. Pornography that links sex to _____ increases men's tolerance of sexual
    aggression. (p. 224)

21. Sexual pressures are typically initiated by those in _____ positions.
    (p. 226)

22. _____ and _____ describe your biological sex, while _____ and _____ are socially constructed terms. (p. 227)

23. Gender is a(n) _____ relationship which is constantly redefined and negotiated. (p. 227)

24. Where sex-linked traits are found, the data reported are for _____ differences. (p. 229)

25. In _____ societies power differentials between women and men are narrowed and women have roles in nonfamily forums. (p. 230)

26. Since there does not seem to be any innate abilities that lead to gender stratification, the causes are most probably located in _____ _____. (p. 230)

27. The _____ perspective views gender inequality as reflecting the distribution by sex of traits required for group survival. (p. 231)

28. Among ways to control women, the most powerful is the responsibility women have for _____. (p. 232)

29. Lowered _____-_____ is a logical consequence of carrying out roles that have little power. (p. 234)

30. Business is stratified by _____ and _____. (p. 236)

31. Few women today have high prestige as a function of their _____. (p. 237)

32. When women move into a previously male dominated field, the men move out and the occupation is _____. (p. 238)

33. Because occupations are _____ segregated, different pay scales can easily be justified by employers. (p. 241)

34. The key variable in actually attending college is the _____ _____. (p. 242)

35. The area in which changes in men's roles have had the most impact is _____ _____. (p. 246)

True-False Questions

*Circle **T** if the statement is true. Circle **F** if the statement is false.*

T   F   1.   Accepted and forbidden sexual behaviors vary culturally and historically. (p. 208)

T   F   2.   Sexual identity is socially constructed and controlled. (p. 208)

T   F   3.   Women's sexual scripts have changed during this century because of changes in women's overall educational levels. (p. 211)

T   F   4.   Surveys indicate that almost half of women sampled have been sexually abused in childhood. (p. 212)

T   F   5.   The rate at which teenagers become sexually active has leveled off and is likely to decrease in the near future. (p. 213)

T   F   6.   The higher the educational and income level of a teenager's family, the *less* likely that teen is to become an adolescent parent. (p. 215)

T   F   7.   Nowhere in the world is homosexuality highly valued behavior. (p. 218)

T   F   8.   The Gay Rights Movement began in the 1960s along with efforts to extend full rights to women, African-Americans, and students. (p. 219)

T   F   9.   The most striking gains in homosexual equality issues took place in the 1980s. (pp. 219, 220)

T   F   10.   The AIDS epidemic coincided with a conservative backlash in the United States which has resulted in increased homophobia. (p. 220)

T   F   11.   The definition of "normal" sexual behavior is up to each individual state. (p. 220)

T   F   12.   Gay men who hide their sexual identities tend to hold "masculine jobs." (p. 220)

T   F   13.   Between five to ten percent of the male population is homosexual. (p. 222)

T   F   14.   More men are bisexual than are women. (p. 222)

T   F   15.   Bisexuality is so emotionally costly that people usually are pushed into either a heterosexual or homosexual lifestyle. (p. 222)

T   F   16.   Typically, homosexual women and men recreate the gender role differences found in the rest of society. (p. 222)

T   F   17.   The majority of homosexuals seek stable relationships. (p. 222)

T   F   18.   When children are abused in child daycare centers, abuses can be viewed as just punishment for women who abandon their domestic duties. (pp. 223, 224)

T   F   19.   The likelihood of being a victim of sexual assault is fairly low. (p. 224)

T   F   20.   It is the sexual component in pornography, not the violence, that invites censorship calls from religious and political conservatives. (p. 224)

T   F   21.   Maleness and femaleness are *achieved* characteristics. (p. 227)

T   F   22.   When high birth rates are needed for societal survival, women must be socialized to nurturing tasks. (p. 230)

T   F   23.   The conflict perspective views the inequality between women and men as socially constructed and not the result of nature. (p. 231)

T   F   24.   Differential socialization will be hard to change because it is rooted in our nature. (p. 233)

T   F   25.   Older people who live in small southern towns and hold blue-collar jobs are the *least* accepting of women political candidates. (p. 235)

T   F   26.   Women's political gains have been at the federal level of power. (p. 235)

T   F   27.   The fact that men still feel uncomfortable in dealing with women hinders women's upward mobility in business. (p. 237)

T   F   28.   The higher the prestige rank of the occupation, the higher the number of men. (p. 238)

T   F   29.   The participation of women in the labor force is a fairly recent trend. (pp. 228, 239)

T   F   30.   Full-time motherhood has always been a luxury. (p. 239)

T   F   31.   While women's participation in the work force has risen, men's participation has declined. (p. 240)

T   F   32.   The gender wage gap is *narrowest* among middle-age women in managerial positions. (p. 241)

T   F   33.   Some gender differences in going to college may be due to testing bias. (p. 242)

T   F   34.   Once in college, female students do not perform as well as male students. (p. 242)

T   F   35.   The content of many fields of study, including history, has been challenged by male and female feminist scholars. (p. 248)

Matching Questions

Match the items in Column B with the correct answer in Column A.

<table>
<tr><td colspan="2">COLUMN A</td><td colspan="2">COLUMN B</td></tr>
<tr><td>1.</td><td>functional perspective (p. 208)</td><td>a.</td><td>Ordinances in San Francisco and New York which extend some civil rights to homosexual and nonmarried hetero-sexual couples.</td></tr>
<tr><td>2.</td><td>sexual harassment (p. 226)</td><td>b.</td><td>Public acknowledgement of a homo-sexual identity.</td></tr>
<tr><td>3.</td><td>reasons for teen pregnancies (p. 215)</td><td>c.</td><td>Any deliberate, repeated, or unwelcome verbal comments, gestures, or physical contacts of a sexual nature.</td></tr>
<tr><td>4.</td><td>"come out" (p. 219)</td><td>d.</td><td>In the large cities, these offer support and protection; often are centered in bars.</td></tr>
<tr><td>5.</td><td>sexual scripts (p. 209)</td><td>e.</td><td>Allows us to organize sexual perceptions and experiences into recognizable patterns.</td></tr>
<tr><td>6.</td><td>bisexual (p. 222)</td><td>f.</td><td>Refers to individuals capable of homo-sexual and heterosexual relationships.</td></tr>
<tr><td>7.</td><td>berdaches (p. 218)</td><td>g.</td><td>Lack of birth control knowledge and lack of access to low-cost family plan-ning services.</td></tr>
<tr><td>8.</td><td>*in vitro* fertilization (p. 218)</td><td>h.</td><td>A third sex; they were thought by native American tribes to have supernatural powers and were treated as guardians of the culture.</td></tr>
<tr><td>9.</td><td>"domestic partners" (p. 223)</td><td>i.</td><td>Conception in a laboratory.</td></tr>
<tr><td>10.</td><td>homosexual subcultures (p. 219)</td><td>j.</td><td>Sexuality is viewed as a powerful drive, rooted in biology but not determined by it, that must be contained and channeled into socially productive directions.</td></tr>
<tr><td>11.</td><td>patriarchy (p. 230)</td><td>k.</td><td>These shape how the mind processes information.</td></tr>
<tr><td>12.</td><td>gender wage gap (p. 241)</td><td>l.</td><td>Refers to a differential in what men and women earn, with women earning less than men.</td></tr>
<tr><td>13.</td><td>gender inequality (p. 234)</td><td>m.</td><td>Refers to the differences between men and women in the distribution of societal re-sources of power, prestige, and property.</td></tr>
<tr><td>14.</td><td>gender stratification (p. 227)</td><td>n.</td><td>The differential evaluation of people's so-cial worth on the basis of biological sex.</td></tr>
<tr><td>15.</td><td>cognitive structures (p. 233)</td><td>o.</td><td>Refers to male dominance.</td></tr>
</table>

ANSWERS

Answers to Fill-In Questions

1. sexual identity
2. children
3. nonsexual
4. reproduction
5. privatization
6. self-esteem
7. pregnancy
8. African-American
9. United States
10. inborn
11. conservatives
12. female
13. learned
14. totality
15. egalitarian
16. heterosexual
17. powerless
18. publicized
19. power
20. violence
21. superior
22. male; female; masculine; feminine
23. power
24. group or collective
25. egalitarian
26. social arrangements
27. functionalist
28. children
29. self-esteem
30. race; gender
31. employment
32. redefined
33. sex
34. parents' resources
35. child care

Answers to True-False Questions

1.	T	10.	T	19.	F	28.	T
2.	T	11.	T	20.	T	29.	F
3.	F	12.	T	21.	F	30.	T
4.	T	13.	T	22.	T	31.	T
5.	F	14.	F	23.	T	32.	F
6.	T	15.	T	24.	F	33.	T
7.	F	16.	F	25.	T	34.	F
8.	T	17.	T	26.	F	35.	T
9.	F	18.	T	27.	T		

Answers to Matching Questions

1.	j	6.	f	11.	o
2.	c	7.	h	12.	l
3.	g	8.	i	13.	m
4.	b	9.	a	14.	n
5.	e	10.	d	15.	k

EXERCISE #1

You read in this chapter that homosexuality occurs all over the world and has occurred throughout history. While most homosexuality in the United States among males occurs between adult men who engage in otherwise conventional roles, the most common homosexual form, cross-culturally, involves a relationship between an adult man and a boy. Not much is known about lesbianism on a cross-cultural basis. The vast majority of homosexuals form long-lasting relationships, and this is especially true for lesbians.

No one really knows what causes homosexuality. The incidence of homosexuality has varied over time and from place to place. At various times in various places, homosexuality has been tolerated, rejected, or even encouraged. Biological factors have not been identified as causing homosexuality, and neither have family patterns nor childhood experiences. Since sexual behavior is learned, it is quite likely that there is a strong element of social learning that takes place for homosexuality.

1. List four myths you have heard about homosexuality.

    A.

    B.

    C.

    D.

2. Explain, sociologically, why you think our society's attitudes towards homosexuality has been so negative.

EXERCISE #2

Rape is a violent crime that is not carried out by "sick" men who lack other sexual outlets. Instead, rape is an act of violence that often is planned out in advance. Rapes often go unreported because women are afraid they will somehow be blamed or because they are reluctant to face further trauma from a medical examination, police questioning, and difficult courtroom lawyers. Rapes often are committed by an acquaintance of the victim. Laws in some states now recognize that husbands may be guilty of raping their wives or that boyfriends may be guilty of raping girlfriends. "Date rape" is sometimes not recognized by the public as real rape. Have you ever heard someone say, "She asked for it?"

Some cultures have no occurrence of rape. Rape tends to depend on cultural factors including a subordinate role for women with accompanying low status, and encouragement of aggression in men.

1. In the United States, identify at least two cultural factors relevant to rape.

    A.

    B.

EXERCISE #3

Think about the expressions we use that are associated with masculinity and femininity. Male students in high school are called "young men" whereas women, no matter what their age, are referred to as "girls." The symbolic communication we call language controls thought and behavior.

1. List two expressions we typically associate with masculinity and femininity, in addition to the above example.

    Masculinity   **Femininity**

    A.

    B.

2. Discuss how we associate masculinity with strength and maturity and femininity with weakness and immaturity. Use your examples as illustrations.

CHAPTER 8
Racial, Ethnic, and Religious Minorities

LEARNING OBJECTIVES

After reading Chapter 8, you should be able to:

1. Compare and contrast cultural homogeneity and cultural heterogeneity, then list the elements of minority group status.

2. Recognize the differences among ethnic, religious, and racial groups, then differentiate the melting pot model and a model of cultural pluralism.

3. Discuss how various minorities have responded to the process of segregation, accommodation, acculturation, assimilation, and amalgamation as they have struggled to become part of the dominant society.

4. Explain the major barriers to integration: prejudice, discrimination, and institutional racism.

5. Trace the impact and ramification of immigration to the United States.

6. Describe the racial minorities in the United States: Native Americans, African-Americans, and Asians.

7. Summarize the similarities and differences among Spanish speaking minorities.

8. Identify the internal stratification of religious minorities: Protestants, Catholics, and Jews.

9. Explain why minorities clash instead of working together to solve the problems of prejudice and discrimination.

GLOSSARY CONCEPTS

cultural homogeneity (p. 252)

cultural heterogeneity (p. 252)

dominant groups (p. 252)

minority-group status (p. 253)

ethnicity (p. 253)

religion (p. 254)

race (p. 254)

melting pot model (p. 255)

triple melting pot (p. 255)

cultural pluralism (p. 255)

segregation (p. 256)

de jure segregation (p. 256)

de facto segregation (p. 256)

accommodation (p. 257)

acculturation (p. 257)

assimilation (p. 257)

amalgamation (p. 258)

prejudice (p. 258)

stereotypical (p. 258)

scapegoating (p. 258)

discrimination (p. 259)

institutionalized discrimination (p. 261)

redlining (p. 261)

genocide (p. 262)

REVIEW QUESTIONS

Fill-In Questions

Fill in the blanks in the sentences below with the correct word or items.

1. Denmark, Sweden, and Norway are examples of nations which are culturally _____ because people in these societies are similar in the language they speak, religious observance, and country of origin. (p. 252)

2. _____ groups exercise control over societal resources and have the power to define standards of beauty and worth. (p. 252)

3. Members of minority groups form _____. (p. 253)

4. The _____ _____ _____ _____ is the most crucial in defining race. (p. 254)

5. Ascribed statuses often serve as _____ boundaries which limit entry into mainstream positions of prestige and power. (p. 254)

6. The _____ _____ pot suggested that ethnic differences were melting but religious differences were not. (p. 255)

7. De _____ segregation is the result of custom and personal choices, while de _____ segregation is supported by law. (p. 256)

8. _____ occurs when people from minority groups are accepted in major social institutions and more personal settings. (p. 257)

9. The process most closely associated with the melting pot is _____, or the mixing of minority and dominant groups through intermarriage. (p. 258)

10. The three barriers to the integration of minority groups are _____, _____, and _____ _____. (p. 258)

11. The most extreme result of prejudice and discrimination is _____, which is the deliberate attempt to murder an entire category of people. (p. 262)

12. A positive consequence of prejudice and discrimination is that social _____ is built for the dominant group. (p. 262)

13. _____-_____ are more likely than whites to develop cancers, diabetes, and get little prenatal care in the first trimester of pregnancy. (p. 269)

14. Evidence supports a _____ model of stratification in the United States. (p. 270)

15. The non-white minority which has established as secure an economic position as have whites is the _____ (p. 273)

16. The four major ethnic divisions of Spanish-speaking people are: Cubans, _____ _____, South Americans and Mexican-Americans. (p. 277)

17. Differences among Spanish-speaking minorities are most striking in terms of _____ and education. (p. 277)

18. Distinctly Mexican neighborhoods are termed _____. (p. 277)

19.   For the Mexican male _____ is the demonstration of physical and sexual powers and the basis of self-respect. (p. 279)

20.   The one common denominator of Middle-Easterners is their Middle-East _____. (p. 280)

21.   The internal status system among American Catholics is headed by _____. (p. 281)

22.   The religious group with the lowest divorce rate and the fewest number of children is _____. (p. 283)

23.   A(n) _____-_____ situation is one in which a group's gain is at another group's expense. (p. 283)

True-False Questions

*Circle **T** if the statement below is true. Circle **F** if the statement is false.*

T   F   1.   Israel and the Soviet Union are societies which are prime examples of culturally homogeneous societies. (p. 252)

T   F   2.   The dominant group in a society is numerically larger than the minority group. (p. 252)

T   F   3.   Based on phenotype and genotype, there are no pure races. (p. 254)

T   F   4.   The triple melting pot was short-lived. (p. 255)

T   F   5.   Cultural pluralism implies an acceptance of various differences in personal matters. (p. 256)

T   F   6.   Stereotypes provide mental shortcuts. (p. 258)

T   F   7.   Prejudice is one of the few attitudes we do not learn. (p. 258)

T   F   8.   If you are prejudiced, you will act in a discriminatory fashion. (p. 259)

T   F   9.   Victims of prejudice and discrimination often have low self-esteem. (p. 260)

T   F   10.   Many disadvantaged whites maintain self-esteem through minority group hatred. (p. 261)

T   F   11.   Functionalists see prejudice and discrimination as having both positive and negative consequences in society. (p. 262)

T   F   12.   The Native American population is growing at a faster rate than the U.S. population. (p. 266)

T   F   13.   African-Americans are *less* likely to vote than are whites. (p. 266)

T F 14. The Indochinese have achieved economic control over produce agriculture, which accounts for their economic successes. (p. 275)

T F 15. Recent Indochinese immigrants have had little in the way of occupational skills and knowledge of English. (pp. 275, 276)

T F 16. It is likely Latinos will outnumber African-Americans as the largest minority group in the United States. (p. 277)

T F 17. Most Mexican-Americans today work on farms. (p. 278)

T F 18. Puerto Ricans came to the mainland in the 1950s in large numbers because of a famine. (p. 279)

T F 19. Tensions among Middle Easterners are caused by drinking, language, and dating. (p. 281)

T F 20. Most Protestants marry other Protestants. (p. 281)

T F 21. The most common route of success for Jews is to go up the corporate ladder. (p. 283)

T F 22. Coalitions among minority groups are rare. (p. 283)

Matching Questions

Match the items in Column B with the correct answer in Column A (columns continue on next page).

COLUMN A

1. minority-group status (p. 252)

2. ethnic hegemony (p. 273)

3. cultural heterogeneity (p. 252)

4. discrimination (p. 259)

5. institutional racism (p. 261)

6. melting-pot model (p. 255)

7. Native Americans (p. 266)

8. stereotypical thinking (p. 258)

COLUMN B

a. Assumes that immigrants will lose their cultural uniqueness and become part of the dominant American culture.

b. The practice by banks and other leading institutions of refusing to make mortgage money available for housing in certain neighborhoods.

c. The poorest and most disadvantaged of all racial or ethnic groups.

d. A social construction; based on the distribution of biological traits.

e. Refers to national background.

f. Involves invisible traits, differential treatment, self-image, and shared identity.

g. Refers to power exerted by one ethnic group over another.

COLUMN A	COLUMN B

COLUMN A

9. race (p. 254)

10. acculturation (p. 257)

11. ethnicity (p. 253)

12. accommodation (p. 257)

13. redlining (p. 261)

COLUMN B

h. Occurs when a society contains a variety of minority groups.

i. Occurs when discrimination is built into normative structures and reinforced by formal and informal agents of social control.

j. Takes place when minority group members adopt the dominant values and norms but are not admitted to intimate groupings.

k. Occurs when the members of a minority group are aware of dominant norms and values without having internalized them.

l. Occurs when a set of characteristics is attributed to all members of a social group.

m. The practice of unequal treatment.

ANSWERS
Answers to Fill-In Questions

1. homogeneous
2. dominant
3. subsocieties
4. definition of the situation
5. caste
6. triple melting
7. facto; jure
8. assimilation
9. amalgamation
10. prejudice, discrimination, institutional racism
11. genocide
12. solidarity
13. African-Americans
14. caste
15. Japanese
16. Puerto Ricans
17. income
18. barrios
19. machismo
20. origin
21. Irish
22. Jews
23. zero-sum

Answers to True-False Questions

1. F
2. F
3. T
4. T
5. T
6. T
7. F
8. F
9. T
10. T
11. T
12. T
13. T
14. F
15. T
16. T
17. F
18. F
19. T
20. T
21. F
22. T

Answers to Matching Questions

1. f
2. g
3. h
4. m
5. i
6. a
7. c
8. l
9. d
10. j
11. e
12. k
13. b

EXERCISE #1

1. Think of some stereotypes you have heard or grew up with about minorities.

<u>**Stereotype**</u>   <u>**Minority**</u>

    A.

    B.

    C.

    D.

    E.

2. Find three examples of advertisements or cartoons from magazines, newspapers, or television which negate or support these stereotypes. Describe what you find (include your source), and report at whom the stereotype is directed.

    A.

    B.

    C.

EXERCISE #2

The authors state that Spanish-speaking Americans may one day outnumber African-Americans as the largest minority in the United States. Yet Latinos are rarely shown on television in dramas or situation comedies. They must learn English in school. In some cities they represent a majority of the population but are not proportionately represented on the police department or in local government.

1.   Name and describe a commercial, drama, or situation comedy in which Latinos appear, or have appeared.

    A.   Is the character(s) represented favorably or negatively? What is the message to the public in the representation?

    B.   Think about any program you enjoy. Describe how the program would change if one of the major characters were Latino.

2.   If you were a non-Latino school board member, what arguments would you put forward to insist that all children use English during school?

3.   If you were a Latino parent, why might you push for bilingual education?

4.   As a prominent, leading Latino citizen of your community, you are to address the city commission to argue for equal Latino representation in all city departments, including police and fire. Make your case convincing and believable.

CHAPTER 9
Courtship, Marriage, and the Family

LEARNING OBJECTIVES

After reading Chapter 9, you should be able to:

1. Explain the origins of the family and appreciate the cross-cultural significance of mate selection and family patterns.

2. Compare the extended and nuclear family systems and trace the historical development of the American family.

3. Characterize the modern family in the United States by focusing on romantic love, mate selection, the marriage market and egalitarianism.

4. Examine the family through the later stages in the life cycle.

5. Discuss the basis for family violence and list the reasons why it occurs.

6. Delineate the factors which account for divorce and the stability of marriages.

7. Compare and contrast the structure and characteristics of Latino and African-American families.

8. Explore alternative family life-styles by focusing on the never-married, cohabitation, childlessness, single-parent households, dual-earner families, homosexual relationships, and men in families.

GLOSSARY CONCEPTS

incest taboo (p. 302)
reciprocity (p. 303)
social fatherhood (p. 303)
extended family (p. 304)
polygamy (p. 305)
nuclear family (p. 305)
romantic love syndrome (p. 307)
homogamy (p. 307)
heterogamy (p. 308)
egalitarianism (p. 309)

empty nest stage (p. 311)
blended family (p. 320)
familism (p. 321)
matrifocal (p. 321)
cohabitation (p. 324)
involuntary childlessness (p. 324)
voluntary childlessness (p. 325)
dual-earner (p. 327)
dual-career families (p. 330)
commuter marriages (p. 331)

REVIEW QUESTIONS

Fill-In Questions

Fill in the blanks in the sentences below with the correct word or item.

1. The original social relationship may have been the _____ of brides and grooms. (p. 303)

2. _____ _____ often are used to keep property within a given kinship line. (p. 303)

3. The _____ family would describe Mr. and Mrs. Conners and their five dependent children. (p. 305)

4. Generally, extended families are found most frequently in _____ societies. (p. 305)

5. The modern family today is mostly a _____ unit. (p. 306)

6. A woman's beauty and _____ are the traits most often valued by men in the marriage market. (p. 308)

7. From the _____ perspective, the marriage market has traditionally represented a mutually beneficial exchange. (p. 308)

8. Women's relative power in the marriage market has increased in recent years because of their ability to be _____ _____. (p. 309)

9. _____ refers to reduced power differences between husbands and wives and between parents and children. (p. 309)

10. In marriage, women's power is highest in societies where _____ passes through the female line and where _____ families predominate. (pp. 309 and 310)

11. Small families represent the dominant United States ideology of _____ and self-fulfillment. (p. 312)

12. When comparing married men with married women, women's rates of mental distress are _____. (p. 314)

13. The most common victims of family violence are _____ and _____. (p. 314)

14. The basic issue in domestic violence is the pattern and structure of family _____ and not a personal problem of the abuser or victim. (pp. 314, 315)

15. Family violence is a complex response to _____-level factors as well as to the _____ _____ of the family. (p. 296)

16. As divorce becomes more _____, it becomes more acceptable. (p. 317)

17. Once a couple marries, the most important predictor of continued stability is the _____ of the marriage. (p. 317)

18. The end of a marriage has especially negative consequences for _____ and _____. (p. 317)

19. Ethnic and minority families are often characterized by _____ households which are a reflection of economic conditions. (p. 320)

20. _____-_____ are more likely than others to never marry or postpone marriage. (p. 321)

21. Lack of _____ depresses marriage rates among the poor. (p. 321)

22. Middle-class African-American marriages are more _____ than their white, dual-earner counterparts. (p. 322)

23. The fastest growing category of single inhabitants is the _____. (p. 324)

24. Cohabitation always has been most common among the less _____.
    (p. 324)

25. The only variable upon which cohabitors and their non-cohabitating age peers differ is
    _____. (p. 324)

26. The involuntarily childless may feel _____ since it is a norm in this
    society to have children. (p. 325)

27. The most severe problem in single-parent families is _____
    _____. (p. 325)

28. _____'s employment has no negative effects on children. (p. 329)

29. A benefit of commuter marriages is the great flexibility in negotiating _____
    _____. (p. 331)

True-False Questions

Circle T if the statement is true. Circle F if the statement is false.

T   F   1.   Family life is socially constructed. (p. 301)

T   F   2.   Incest rules may be the foundation of the family. (p. 302)

T   F   3.   Marriage rituals are universal because the entire society has a stake in orderly
                 reproduction. (p. 304)

T   F   4.   Nuclear families are characteristic in many simple societies. (p. 305)

T   F   5.   The extended family used to be most dominant in the United States. (p. 306)

T   F   6.   Most extended families in the past and today, are a matter of temporary
                 adjustments. (p. 306)

T   F   7.   Even today, marriage is too important to families and societies to be left entirely
                 to an engaged couple. (p. 307)

T   F   8.   Social class is an important feature of the marriage market. (p. 308)

T   F   9.   The idea of the emotionally priceless child of the late nineteenth century has
                 been replaced with the idea of the economically valuable child of today.
                 (p. 311)

T   F   10.   Small families result in fewer sources of social support for the parents in old
                 age. (p. 312)

T   F   11.   Today, improvements in the economy means earlier marriage and parenthood
                 than they've meant in past years. (p. 312)

T   F   12.   Currently, high divorce rates largely reflect the high marriage rates since World War II. (p. 313)

T   F   13.   Social surveys record high rates of unhappiness in American marriages. (p. 313)

T   F   14.   Conflict theorists assume a harmony of interests within the family. (p. 313)

T   F   15.   Family violence is more characteristic of families associated with the military or who are deeply religious. (p. 315)

T   F   16.   The vast majority of abused wives are helpless victims who cannot change their lives. (p. 316)

T   F   17.   Parental death has a stronger effect on children's emotional well-being than divorce. (p. 317)

T   F   18.   Having sons reduces the likelihood of divorce. (p. 317)

T   F   19.   The effects of divorce are stronger for boys than for girls. (pp. 317, 318)

T   F   20.   Children adjust better to divorce when the father remains in close contact. (p. 318)

T   F   21.   Most divorced people remarry. (p. 318)

T   F   22.   Almost three-fourths of all African-American families are headed by women. (p. 321)

T   F   23.   The reason so many people choose to live alone and never marry is because of value changes in our society. (p. 323)

T   F   24.   Most singles live lives very different from their married counterparts. (p. 323)

T   F   25.   Cohabitors have significantly *lower* divorce rates than do non-cohabitors. (p. 324)

T   F   26.   Single-parent fathers perform competently as parents and have higher incomes than divorced mothers. (p. 327)

T   F   27.   Dual-earner marriages are more stable than marriages with just one wage earner. (p. 328)

T   F   28.   For both women employed in *and* out of the home, their husbands are doing more housework. (p. 328)

T   F   29.   The "new father" is one who participates in the birthing process and so bonds immediately with the child. (p. 331)

Matching Questions

Match items in Column B with the correct answer in Column A.

COLUMN A	COLUMN B
1. matrifocal (p. 321)	a. Occurs when persons of the opposite sex share living quarters.
2. empty nest (p. 311)	b. Creates extended households composed of a person with more than one marriage partner.
3. blended families (p. 320)	c. Refers to family closeness, traditionalism, and male dominance.
4 extended families (p. 304)	d. This forbids sexual relations between certain group members.
5. cohabitation (p. 324)	e. The tendency to select a mate with different social background characteristics.
6. reciprocity (p. 303)	f. Stage of the family life cycle when all children are out of the house and the parents are alone together again.
7. familism (p. 321)	g. The tendency to select a mate with similar social background characteristics.
8. social father (p. 303)	h. A long courtship was typical during which the husband-to-be established himself. Economically; the couple would eventually have four children.
9. family violence (p. 315)	i. Realized when people have similar resources.
10. homogamy (p. 307)	j. A large unit composed of several related households, most often involving three or more generations.
11. egalitarianism (p. 309)	k. Refers to families centered on the women.
12. 1900 couple (p. 311)	l. The role of father can be assigned to a specific person in society who is responsible for the protection of a woman and her children.
13. polygamy (p. 305)	m. Consists of children of previous marriages.
14. incest taboo (p. 302)	n. Strongly associated with low educational and occupational status, early marriage and unplanned pregnancy.
15. heterogamy (p. 308)	o. This obligates the receiver of a gift to return something of equivalent value.

ANSWERS
Answers to Fill-In Questions

1. exchange
2. incest taboos
3. nuclear
4. nonindustrial
5. consuming
6. youth
7. functional
8. economically independent
9. egalitarianism
10. property; nuclear
11. individualism
12. higher
13. wives and children
14. authority
15. societal; internal dynamics
16. common
17. length
18. women; children
19. extended
20. African-American
21. employment
22. egalitarian
23. widowed
24. educated
25. religiosity
26. stigmatized
27. low income
28. mother's
29. marital roles

True-False Questions

1. T
2. T
3. T
4. T
5. F
6. T
7. T
8. T
9. F
10. T
11. F
12. T
13. F
14. F
15. T
16. F
17. F
18. T
19. F
20. F
21. T
22. F
23. T
24. F
25. F
26. T
27. F
28. T
29. F

Matching Questions

1. k
2. f
3. m
4. j
5. a
6. o
7. c
8. l
9. n
10. g
11. i
12. h
13. b
14. d
15. e

EXERCISE #1

Amanda and Scott knew each other in the medium-sized town where they grew-up, but did not date one another until they met in a business course during their second year in college. After several months of dating, they got an apartment together during their third year of college. Both chose to maintain separate addresses at college to avoid their parents' disapproval of their living arrangements.

Both are active volunteers in a campus group which networks local retired business people with those who share new, small businesses in the local community. Amanda and Scott want to establish their careers and perhaps seek advanced degrees before marrying and having children. Amanda is not sure she even wants children, but has not discussed this issue with Scott. They have decided that when they do marry, they will marry in the local Protestant Church near their campus because they like the new minister. Amanda and Scott's parents have met and like each other. They hope to find jobs near the campus community where they met, because they enjoy the atmosphere and have friends there.

1.   List all the homogeneous characteristics of the couple.

2.   If Amanda and Scott were to experience problems after marriage, in which areas would those problems likely arise? Why?

EXERCISE #2

You may not have thought about mate selection as a market situation where people "sell" themselves to attract the most pleasing partner possible. Your value in the market is determined by, among other factors, standards of physical attractiveness, age, social class, and occupational status or potential. You are a sociologist who has decided to interview couples who have applied for marriage licenses in order to isolate the factors most important to the couple in the marriage market.

1. From the information you read in Chapter 2, what method in addition to interviewing are you using?

2. List ten questions you would ask the soon-to-be wife and then the soon-to-be husband.

    Questions for Wife   **Questions for Husband**

    A.

    B.

    C.

    D.

    E.

F.

G.

H.

I.

J.

3.   Explain the functional aspects of the marriage market.

4.   Describe how a conflict theorist would explain the marriage market.

CHAPTER 10
Economic and Political Systems

LEARNING OBJECTIVES

After reading Chapter 10, you should be able to:

1. Discuss the origins, history and components of economic systems in terms of a society's mode of subsistence.

2. Examine the continuum of modern economic systems which ranges from economic activity regulated by public agencies to economic activity left to the private sector, and which includes free-enterprise capitalism to socialism.

3. Examine specialization and the division of labor in industrial societies and the role of alienation in the modern work place and understand the nature of automation and the impact it has had on worker satisfaction.

4. Trace the development of the American labor movement and list the benefits of the American labor movement for workers and the criticisms of this movement.

5. Differentiate the core sector and the periphery in terms of the dual economy and the split of segmented labor market.

6. Explain how employment rates are determined, how trends in employment are likely to affect jobs, and how unemployment affects youth.

7. Review the characteristics of the corporation and analyze its place in the economic system.

109

8. Define power, types of power, and authority.

9. Compare and contrast socialism, democracy, totalitarian and democratic states.

10. Explain the various ways public opinion may be manipulated.

11. Discuss and provide examples of some of the societal consequences of political inequality including Michels' iron law of oligarchy.

12. Identify who in our society votes, who does not, and why and then discuss how people acquire their political attitudes.

13. Compare and contrast explanations of the structure of power in the United States: the power-elite and the pluralist models of political power.

14. Summarize the role of the military in our society today as compared with the past and include the position of women and minorities, then differentiate militarism.

15. Explain the nature of the military-industrial complex and its impact on the economies of the Third World and of the superpowers.

GLOSSARY CONCEPTS

mode of subsistence (p. 335)
institutionalization (p. 335)
economic system (p. 335)
service work (p. 336)
rule of reciprocity (p. 338)
free market system (p. 338)
public agencies (p. 339)
private interests (p. 339)
free-enterprise capitalism (p. 339)
socialistic economic system (p. 339)
welfare or state capitalism (p.340)
monopolization (p. 341)
conglomerates (p. 341)
interlocking corporate directorships (p. 341)
multinational corporations (p. 341)
socialism (p. 341)
democratic or welfare socialism (p. 343)
division of labor (p. 343)
alienation (p. 343)

automation (p. 344)
job autonomy (p. 345)
core sector (p. 348)
periphery (p. 348)
dual economy (p. 349)
split or segmented labor market (p. 349)
authority (p. 354)
traditional authority (p. 354)
charismatic authority (p. 354)
legal-rational or bureaucratic authority (p. 355)
totalitarian regimes (p. 356)
democratic societies (p. 357)
propaganda (p. 358)
censorship (p. 358)
repression (p. 359)
oligarchy (p. 360)
political action committee (p. 361)
political socialization (p. 366)
yuppie (p. 366)

power-elite model (p. 366)
pluralist model (p. 370)
all-volunteer force (p. 371)

militarism (p. 373)
militarization (p. 373)
military-industrial complex (p. 374)

REVIEW QUESTIONS

Fill-In Questions

Fill in the blanks in the sentences below with the correct word or items.

1. The economic system of any society consists of norms and patterned activities regulating _____, _____, and _____ of goods and services. (p. 335)

2. _____ production consists of taking resources directly from the earth and using them without much processing. (p. 336)

3. The simplest means of distributing surplus is by _____ of goods and services judged to be of equivalent value by the traders. (p. 337)

4. Interlocking corporate directorships in the long run decrease _____ and increase _____. (p. 341)

5. Multinational corporations present problems of _____ and control. (p. 341)

6. Welfare socialism involves high rates of _____. (p. 343)

7. Democratic socialism has worked fairly well in reducing inequality in _____ _____, but not as well in the Soviet Union. (p. 343)

8. The central social structure of industrialism is the _____ (p. 343)

9. Worker _____ is highest in jobs where an employee has some control over the work process and is not closely supervised. (p. 345)

10. The single most important factor in determining the desirability of a job is _____. (p. 345)

11. The interests of workers in the United States have been represented by _____ rather than political parties. (p. 346)

12.   Labor unions in _____ and the United States have been coopted by management and the government. (p. 346)

13.   The strength of American labor unions depends on their willingness to support each other by engaging in sympathy _____. (p. 348)

14.   The only organized force for economic democracy in this country is the _____. (p. 348)

15.   The _____ _____ consists of major industries, whereas the _____ consists of smaller, competitive, low-profit firms using non-union workers. (p. 348)

16.   The _____ _____ is made up of two separate types of firms: core and peripheral. (p. 349)

17.   The _____ _____ market is differentiated by race and gender. (p. 329)

18.   For youth not going to college _____ _____ is the socially acceptable means of achieving adult status. (p. 350)

19.   Corporations often try to soften their public image by making _____ _____ and supporting local causes. (pp. 350, 351)

20.   A(n) _____ is a formal organization that is a legal entity in its own right. (p. 352)

21.   _____ is the exercise of control through legitimated and institutionalized channels, but _____ is the exercise of informal persuasion. (p. 354)

22.   Alexander the Great, Mao, Castro, Joan of Arc, Hitler, and Gandhi are all examples of leaders who enjoyed the type of legitimated power Weber called _____ _____. (p. 354)

23.   The _____ perspective sees the need for internal order and defense against external enemies. (p. 355)

24.   Totalitarianism is most common in societies without important _____ _____ _____. (p. 356)

25.   Wiretapping, direct surveillance, and opening mail are all techniques of _____ _____. (p. 359)

26. Curfews, imprisonment, and house arrest are examples of the use of _____ in suppressing political dissent. (p. 359)

27. The _____ _____ states that because decision makers have a crucial interest in being proven correct, they tend to manipulate information and individuals to gain support. (p. 360)

28. Running for political office, voting, or contributing money to political campaigns are all examples of _____ _____. (p. 360)

29. The fundamental act of political involvement is _____. (p. 362)

30. Voting patterns vary by age, race, ethnicity, and _____. (p. 362)

31. People who have the most to gain from government interventions are the least likely to _____. (p. 363)

32. The subgroup least likely to vote are aged _____ to _____-_____. (p. 363)

33. _____ is a signal that powerless Americans are withdrawing from a political system which does not recognize their needs. (p. 363)

34. The greatest long-term change in voting patterns with impact for the future involves _____. (p. 365)

35. White_____ are likely to vote Democratic and support women candidates. (p. 365)

36. The _____-_____ _____ was conceived as smaller and more professional than a citizen army. (p. 371)

37. The _____ is the most integrated institution in this society, but only at the lower ranks. (p. 372)

38. _____ refers to a societal emphasis on military ideals and virtues and a glorification of war and warriors. (p. 373)

39. The _____-_____ _____ consists of a large permanent military establishment combined with an immense armament industry. (p. 374)

40. The system of "_____ _____" is not well supervised by civilian authorities so cost overruns are common. (p. 374)

True-False Questions

*Circle **T** if the statement below is true. Circie **F** if the statement is false.*

T   F   1.   Being a travel agent would place an individual in a situation of secondary production. (p. 336)

T   F   2.   The United States is becoming a service society. (p. 336)

T   F   3.   Most service sector jobs will be at the high end of the pay scale. (p.336)

T   F   4.   The major method of distribution in complex modern societies is reciprocity. (p. 338)

T   F   5.   The household today is primarily a unit of consumption. (p. 338)

T   F   6.   What motivates workers *and* owners in a capitalist economy is the promise of keeping the fruits of their labor. (p. 340)

T   F   7.   Welfare, or state capitalism, largely is paid for by the working classes. (p. 341)

T   F   8.   Most multinationals fall under the supervision of at least one government. (p. 341)

T   F   9.   Deskilling is characteristic of factory work, but not white collar work. (p. 344)

T   F   10.   Automation can improve a manager's ability to control and supervise employees. (p. 345)

T   F   11.   Most American workers are satisfied with their jobs. (p. 345)

T   F   12.   The white male worker has profited the most from unionization. (p. 347)

T   F   13.   The union of the future must include female service workers and minorities. (p. 348)

T   F   14.   Owners and workers in the periphery have more political power than those in the core sector. (pp. 348, 349)

T   F   15.   Peripheral employees primarily are women and minorities. (p. 349)

T   F   16.   Some involuntary non-workers are engaged in occupations which are illegal but pay high incomes. (p. 350)

T   F   17.   The solution to minority youth unemployment is to guarantee jobs at salaries just above minimum wage levels. (p. 350)

T   F   18.   Corporate power has been challenged by the American public in court since the 1930s. (p. 350)

T   F   19.   The line between ownership and management has come to be blurred in recent years. (p. 352)

T   F   20.   Most authority comes from the *roles* we occupy. (p. 354)

T   F   21.   Much of political sociology today focuses on how certain political leaders obtained their power. (p. 356)

T   F   22.   Dictators are only military leaders. (p. 356)

T   F   23.   What is an important hallmark of democracy is how many people vote. (p. 357)

T   F   24.   When there are extreme economic and power differences in a society and severe measures are used to coerce the population, the society will be stable. (p. 360)

T   F   25.   In any society new rulers are driven to being corrupted by power just as previous rulers were. (p. 360)

T   F   26.   In a democracy the iron law of oligarchy does not function because it is repealed. (p. 345)

T   F   27.   Americans seem to like restrictions on voter registration. (p. 365)

T   F   28.   The vast majority of American presidents were from the power elite. (p. 367)

T   F   29.   A criticism of the power elite model is that it assumes a conflict among leaders that actually does not exist. (pp. 370)

T   F   30.   Recruits who enlist in the AVF are from middle-class families. (p.372)

T   F   31.   In the military members of different races interact together on *and* off duty. (p. 372)

T   F   32.   Educational standards for women in the military are higher than those for men. (p. 372)

T   F   33.   The greatest impact of militarization is the reinforcement of ideas of male superiority. (p. 373)

T   F   34.   Most of our current and future military budget is devoted to military personnel. (p. 374)

T   F   35.   The international trade in food products is *greater* than that in the trade of armaments. (p. 374)

Matching Questions

Match the items in Column B with the correct answer in Column A (columns continue on next page).

COLUMN A

1. workplace democracy (p. 346)

2. automation (p. 344)

3. conglomerate (p. 344)

4. institutionalization (p. 335)

5. quality circle (p. 346)

6. welfare or state capitalism (p. 343)

7. division of labor (p. 343)

8. mode of substance (p. 335)

9. job autonomy (p. 345)

10. alienation (p. 343)

11. rule of reciprocity (p. 338)

12. militarization (p. 373)

13. propaganda (p. 358)

14. nation-state (p. 355)

15. political socialization (p. 366)

16. censorship (p. 358)

17. power-elite model (p. 366)

18. traditional authority (p. 354)

19. totalitarian regimes (p. 356)

COLUMN B

a. Teams of employees and managers meet to discuss how to improve their work performance.

b. An example is the potlatch or the giving of gifts that obligates the receiver to return something of similar value at some later date.

c. The replacement of workers with machines.

d. The separation of work into distinct parts, each of which is performed by an individual or a group.

e. Feelings of powerlessness, normlessness, and being cut off from the product of one's labor.

f. Involves making decisions about the timing and sequence of tasks, exercising judgement, and having an impact on the outcome.

g. One holding company owns controlling interests in other companies in a variety of commercial areas.

h. Employees become the owners.

i. Refers to how the group adapts to its environment.

j. The actual economic system of the U.S. and other industrial societies.

k. The process whereby a given adaptation becomes an established pattern.

l. Occurs when an entire society is mobilized around militaristic goals.

m. There are few restraints on this, it is irrational, and an example is a patriarchy.

n. Special interest organizations that use funds to support causes and candidates.

o. The probability of realizing one's goals regardless of the will of others.

COLUMN A	**COLUMN B**

20. PACs (p. 361)

21. power (p. 354)

22. pluralist model (p. 370)

p. The influences and experiences that lead people to define their political orientation.

q. Assumes that there are many different and competing bases of power.

r. Involves the selective withholding of information.

s. Regulates *all* aspects of society and the people within it.

t. Refers to the selected release of information favorable to those in power and designed to generate high levels of solidarity.

u. Assumes that decision making is concentrated in the hands of a small group.

v. Organized sets of institutions that govern and defend a given territory.

ANSWERS
Answers to Fill-In Questions

1. production; distribution; consumption
2. primary
3. barter
4. competition; profits
5. loyalty
6. taxation
7. Western Europe
8. factory
9. satisfaction
10. income
11. unions
12. Japan
13. strikes
14. union
15. core sector; periphery
16. dual economy
17. split or segmented labor
18. steady employment
19 charitable contributions
20. corporation
21. authority; influence
22. charismatic authority
23. functionalist
24. preconditions of democracies
25. chilling dissent
26. repression
27. iron law
28. political participation
29. voting
30. gender
31. vote
32. eighteen; twenty-four
33. nonvoting
34. women
35. women
36. all-volunteer force
37. army
38. militarism
39. military-industrial complex
40. weapons welfarism

Answers to True-False Questions

1.	F	10.	T	19.	T	28.	T
2.	T	11.	T	20.	F	29.	F
3.	F	12.	T	21.	F	30.	T
4.	F	13.	T	22.	F	31.	F
5.	T	14.	F	23.	F	32.	T
6.	T	15.	T	24.	F	33.	F
7.	T	16.	T	25.	T	34.	F
8.	F	17.	F	26.	F	35.	F
9.	F	18.	F	27.	T		

Answers to Matching Questions

1.	h	7.	d	13.	t	19.	s
2.	c	8.	i	14.	v	20.	n
3.	g	9.	f	15.	p	21.	o
4.	k	10.	e	16.	r	22.	q
5.	a	11.	b	17.	u		
6.	j	12.	l	18.	m		

EXERCISE #1

In local newspapers, news magazines, or the *Wall Street Journal*, find two examples of each of the following:

Illegitimate power	Legitimate power (authority)
Traditional authority	Charismatic authority
Legal-Rational authority	

Attach your articles securely to your Study Guide and include all appropriate bibliographical information. Write a few sentences showing how your article illustrates each of the concepts involved. How did the leaders in your articles get to their positions of power?

Illegitimate power:

Legitimate power (authority):

Traditional authority:

EXERCISE #2

Over the past few decades there has been a dramatic change in the type of work the labor force has engaged in. Many people in the work force are engaging in producing goods and services that did not exist ten years ago.

1. List at least eight products which did not exist ten years ago.

    A.   E.

    B.   F.

    C.   G.

    D.   H.

2. List at least twelve types of service jobs which did not exist ten years ago.

    A.   G.

    B.   H.

    C.   I.

    D.   J.

    E.   K.

    F.   L.

CHAPTER 11
Educational and Religious Systems

LEARNING OBJECTIVES

After reading Chapter 11, you should be able to:

1. Outline the functions of education, and compare and contrast the functional and conflict perspectives of education and explain the features of the American educational system by focusing on structure.

2. Compare public and private school systems in terms of social class ramifications and educational quality, then contrast the experiences, successes, and failures of students in suburban and urban schools, and summarize how teachers can affect their students' achievement.

3. Review the functions and structure of higher education and explain the nature and role of the faculty in higher education.

4. Discuss the characteristics, diversity, and advantages of students attending institutions of higher learning including the impact of race, gender, and social class.

5. Identify the role of the community college in higher education.

6.   Compare the educational goals of quality and equality and their implications for the educational institutions and our society.

7.   Discuss how handicapped students have been served by the educational system and some of the problems with these special programs.

8.   Define belief system and religion and explain how these may arise by examining the ideas of Durkheim and Weber.

9.   Explain what sociologists study about belief systems, list the criteria which define how a belief system exists, delineate the manifest and latent functions of religious rituals and then the dysfunctions of belief systems.

10. Discuss the essential structural components of any religion or ideology and then apply them to Marxism.

11. Present the basic explanations for the varieties of religious experience across time and place by examining the origins of religious belief systems and the reasons for a shift from feminine imagery to male-dominated imagery.

12. Differentiate the sacred and the profane, explain the nature of magic, and examine how religions can support the dual nature of both status quo and social changes as expressed in Max Weber's distinction between the priestly and the prophetic.

13. Review the impact of modernization and secularization on modern religious faith.

14. Describe contemporary trends in religion by examining secularization and mainstreaming religions in the United States, the role of the African-American church, and then differentiate the roles of fundamentalists from that of the evangelicals.

GLOSSARY CONCEPTS

manifest functions (p. 380)
latent functions (p. 380)
hidden curriculum (p. 382)
meritocracy (p. 382)
tracks (p. 383)
cultural capital (p. 383)
post secondary education (p. 385)
inclusive (American education) (p. 385)
parochial schools (p. 387)
preparatory schools (p. 387)
cooperative learning (p. 390)

specialization of knowledge (p. 391)
mainstreaming (p. 401)
voucher system (p. 402)
belief system (p. 404)
religion (p. 404)
secular ideologies (p. 404)
sectarian conflict (p. 406)
origin myth (p. 406)
transcendence (p. 407)
sacred (p. 408)
profane (p. 408)

religious roles (p. 408)
magic (p. 408)
priestly (p. 409)
prophet (p. 409)
routinization of charisma (p. 409)
modernization (p. 411)
secularization (p. 411)

American civil religion (p. 000)
fundamentalism (p. 418)
New Christian Right (p. 419)
evangelical (p. 420)
born again (p. 421)
cults and new religious movements (p. 421)
new age movement (p. 422)

REVIEW QUESTIONS
Fill-In Questions

Fill in the blanks in the sentences below with the correct word or item.

1. In very simple societies, children of both sexes learn skills by _____. (p. 380)

2. When schools provide a babysitting function, sociologists speak of a(n) _____ function, but when children are taught to read and write sociologists talk about a(n) _____ function. (pp. 380 and 381)

3. The job of presenting a common culture has fallen to _____. (p. 381)

4. _____ were to be the melting pots for immigrants who came to this country between 1880 and 1920. (p. 382)

5. _____ _____ is sex-segregated and geared toward working class youth. (p. 382)

6. In the _____ perspective, schools will encourage competition in order to separate the best students from the less able students. (pp. 382, 383)

7. The cultural and educational resources of your _____ determine how long you remain in school and how successfully you perform. (p. 384)

8. Family _____ is an important variable in determining advantages or disadvantages in a child's life. (p. 384)

9. In modern societies, the trend in education has been toward _____ and specialization. (p. 385)

10.   The American educational system is _____, meaning that it is open to almost all children of given ages. (p. 385)

11.   _____ _____ programs emphasize cooperation and group activities whereas middle class preschools stress individualism and relationships to adults. (p. 385)

12.   The two separate school systems in the United States are _____ and _____. (p. 387)

13.   The most extensive parochial school system in this country is operated by the _____ _____ Church. (p. 387)

14.   The fastest growing parochial education system today is run by the _____ _____ school system. (p. 387)

15.   A _____ level topic of education would deal with the functions and structure of the educational system. (p. 388)

16.   In the _____ school, students are bored and divided into subcultures, which work to administrators' advantages. (p. 388)

17.   More effective than ability grouping or competition in raising students performance is _____ _____. (p. 390)

18.   Universities are organized into discrete units because of _____ _____ _____. (p. 376)

19.   College enrollments have dropped sharply for _____-_____ _____, but Asian enrollments have been rising. (p. 393)

20.   Women who attend predominantly _____'s colleges are more likely than graduates of other colleges to achieve higher career accomplishments. (p. 394)

21.   The academic growth industry in the United States since 1970, has been the _____ _____. (p. 396)

22.   The two educational goals which have come into conflict are _____ vs. _____. (p. 397)

23.   _____ schools are designed to attract students by offering specialized educational programs. (p. 399)

24.   _____ _____ divides a school district's students into separate schools for given grade levels. (p. 400)

25. The label of "learning disability" provides _____ for special education teachers and validates this area of study. (p. 401)

26. _____ involves integrating handicapped students into the regular school program. (p. 401)

27. The trend in American education is toward _____. (p. 401)

28. _____ saw religion dependent upon agreement among minds. (p. 404)

29. _____ examined world religions to see how they provided a psychological and practical context for economic activity. (p. 404)

30. Systems of belief and ritual fill _____ and group needs. (p. 405)

31. The _____ is invested in the supernatural while the _____ is part of the earth. (p. 408)

32. Most religions are _____, meaning they support the status quo. (p. 409)

33. The most powerful source of social change is _____. (p. 411)

34. _____ are more likely than other religious groups to say religion is very important. (p. 413)

35. Participation in religious services is highest among _____ and the elderly. (p. 413)

36. African-American churches have been open in _____ roles for women. (p. 415)

37. The Roman Catholic population in this country continues to grow because of immigration of _____. (p. 416)

38. Greatest resistance to women clergy comes from the _____ Church and _____ Jews. (p. 417)

39. _____ believe every word of the Bible is to be taken literally. (p. 418)

40. Fundamentalist leaders have taken advantage of public distress over the failures of _____. (p. 419)

41. _____ refers to an emphasis on the personal witnessing of God's presence. (p. 420)

42. The idea of being _____ _____ is essential to evangelical doctrine. (p. 421)

43. The Unification Church is based on Christianity and strongly supports _____ and the American military. (p. 421)

True-False Questions

*Circle **T** if the statement is true. Circle **F** if the statement is false.*

T   F   1.   In complex societies, schools have the responsibility for promoting group unity, which is a societal goal. (p. 380)

T   F   2.   Between 1880 and 1920 schools were not too successful as avenues of mobility but today, because of changed social conditions, schools successfully function in this way. (p. 382)

T   F   3.   An assumption of a meritocracy is that standardized tests are a means for identifying bright and less able students. (p. 383)

T   F   4.   Conflict, but not the functionalist perspective, views education as a filtering process which channels children into academic careers. (p. 383)

T   F   5.   Tracks often coincide with social class backgrounds. (p. 383)

T   F   6.   Poorer parents tend to transmit culture capital to their children. (pp. 383, 384)

T   F   7.   Two-parent households convey higher expectations of children than do single-parent households. (p. 384)

T   F   8.   More Americans have been to college than the citizens of any other country in the world. (p. 385)

T   F   9.   Cognitive differences by race are the result of innate abilities and not life-style factors. (p. 386)

T   F   10.   The initial effort to "professionalize" schools between 1870 and 1940 was a huge success in urban and rural schools. (p. 387)

T   F   11.   Long-term economic disadvantages for Latino students are due, in part, to literacy rates. (p. 389)

T   F   12.   Teachers treat boys and girls differently in school. (p. 390)

T   F   13.   The Carnegie Corporation report encourages schools to reinstate tracking, small schools, and special needs' education. (p. 390)

T   F   14.   Teaching skills are important determinants of the academic rank of professors in universities. (p. 392)

T   F   15.   College teaching is not a financially attractive choice for minorities. (p. 392)

T   F   16.   More African-Americans attend two-year colleges rather than four-year colleges. (p. 394)

T   F   17.   Attendance at less prestigious universities and colleges mean a lower quality education for low- or moderate-income students. (p. 395)

T   F   18.   Attending college in the United States has more to do with high school grades than family income. (p. 396)

T   F   19.   Community colleges limit some students' opportunities. (p. 397)

T   F   20.   Racial segregation in schools has decreased since 1970. (p. 397)

T   F   21.   When school desegregation is accompanied by busing, local opposition is especially strong. (p. 399)

T   F   22.   Integration methods involve magnet schools, grade differentiation, and merging school districts. (pp. 399, 400)

T   F   23.   Currently, federal law requires individual school districts to educate only competent students. (p. 400)

T   F   24.   To the sociologist, the context of religion is not important so long as the ideas and rituals reduce individual anxiety and promote cohesion. (p. 405)

T   F   25.   Sacredness is a characteristic imposed by a group. (p. 408)

T   F   26.   The priestly functions often are at odds with the established order. (p. 409)

T   F   27.   Science is the greatest challenge to traditional religious faith. (pp. 411 , 412)

T   F   28.   Attendance at religious services has risen since the 1970s. (p. 413)

T   F   29.   We make secular holidays sacred in the tradition of American civil religion. (p. 414)

T   F   30.   Most African-Americans are Baptist. (p. 414)

T   F   31.   Mainstream churches have had a *decline* in membership. (p. 415)

T   F   32.   Fundamentalist revivals describe trends within Protestant churches and not within the Catholic Church. (p. 419)

T   F   33.   Fundamentalist Protestant churches have never supported a separation between church and state. (p. 420)

T   F   34.   There are many fundamentalists who do not insist on a literal interpretation of the Bible as do the evangelicals. (p. 421)

T   F   35.   The fastest growing cult today that attracts older adults is the Church of Scientology. (p. 422)

Matching Questions

Match the items in Column B with the correct answer in Column A.

COLUMN A	COLUMN B
1. culture capital (p. 383)	a. Low tuition, evening courses, part-time programs, convenient locations.
2. meritocracy (p. 382)	b. Private schools which prepare the children of well-off parents for entry into elite colleges.
3. community college advantages (p. 397)	c. Programs of varying content and pacing, to which students are assigned.
4. hidden curriculum (p. 382)	d. Refers to the unannounced lessons learned at school, such as ethnocentrism and respect for authority.
5. tracks (p. 383)	e. Occurs when students pool their talents and help one another.
6. preparatory schools (p. 387)	f. A hierarchy of talent in which rewards are based on ability and credentials.
7. cooperative learning (p. 390)	g. Refers to a style of talking and thinking as well as an interest in the arts which permits people to feel comfortable in the dominant culture and in educational settings.
8. origin myth (p. 406)	
9. magic (p. 408)	h. A set of shared ideas about the meaning of life.
10. secular ideology (p. 404)	i. A set of unifying beliefs that sees America as divinely blessed, with a moral mission and guided by ethical standards.
11. sectarian conflict (p. 406)	
12. transcendence (p. 407)	j. A charismatic figure, witnessing a revelation calling for a new order.
13. prophet (p. 409)	k. Refers to the need to go beyond the limits of one's own senses and feel that life has meaning beyond one's daily experiences.
14. belief system (p. 404)	l. Behavior designed to manipulate unseen forces.
15. American civil religion (p. 414)	m. Interreligious strife which the U.S. has avoided.
16. Roman Catholics (p. 413)	n. The single largest body of religious believers in the United States.
17. ecclesia (p. 412)	o. Belief systems based on worldly rather than supernatural forces.
	p. A story of how a group begins.
	q. An "official" church to which all members of a society belong.

ANSWERS
Answers to Fill-In Questions

1.	imitation	16.	suburban	31.	sacred; profane
2.	latent; manifest	17.	cooperative learning	32.	conservative
3.	textbooks	18.	specialization of knowledge	33.	modernization
4.	schools	19.	African-American men	34.	Protestants
5.	vocational education	20.	women's	35	women
6.	functionalist	21.	community college	36.	leadership
7.	family	22.	quality; equality	37.	Latinos
8.	size	23.	magnet	38.	Catholic; Orthodox
9.	differentiation	24.	grade differentiation	39.	fundamentalists
10.	inclusive	25.	employment	40.	modernism
11.	Head Start	26.	mainstreaming	41.	evangelicalism
12.	public; private	27.	pluralism	42.	born again
13.	Roman Catholic	28.	Durkheim	43.	capitalism
14.	American Christian	29.	Weber		
15.	macro	30.	individual		

Answers to True-False Questions

1.	T	10.	F	19.	T	28.	F
2.	F	11.	T	20.	F	29.	T
3.	T	12.	T	21.	T	30.	T
4.	F	13.	F	22.	T	31.	T
5.	T	14.	F	23.	F	32.	F
6.	F	15.	T	24.	T	33.	T
7.	T	16.	T	25.	T	34.	F
8.	T	17.	F	26.	F	35.	F
9.	F	18.	F	27.	F		

Answers to Matching Questions

1.	g	7.	e	13.	j
2.	f	8.	p	14.	h
3.	a	9.	l	15.	i
4.	d	10.	o	16.	n
5.	c	11.	m	17.	q
6.	b	12.	k		

EXERCISE #1

A popular exercise in many communities could be called "Blame Public Schools for Problems." Parents and other adults in some communities blame the public schools for all kinds of social and individual problems. Schools sometimes blame the community for not passing levies designed to raise money to support extracurricular activities, sports, and maintenance programs. Students often blame teachers, administrators, and parents for the problems they encounter.

1.   Identify three *social problems* you believe are popularly associated with public schools.

A.

B.

C.

2.   Why do parents, students, and the community tend to blame public schools for the social problems you identified? Be specific.

3.   If you need to, reread the section in Chapter One on the sociological imagination. Then identify three *private* issues which are associated with *public* ones.

Private	**Public**

A.

B.

C.

4.   As a sociologist, you are asked to explain or justify the connection between the private and public issues you cited above. What are you going to say for each issue?

A.

B.

C.

5. How would you, as a sociologist, go about ending the game, "Blame Public Schools for Problems"?

EXERCISE #2

Denominations, sects, and cults have a long history in the U.S. Denominations are well-established, and are typical of mainstream churches. They are fairly tolerant of other religions and are characterized by bureaucratic organizations with well-educated clergy. Sects usually split off from denominations, and people become members through an emotional conversion. Oftentimes, religious services try to recapture the emotional thrill of the conversion experience. Cults frequency have little to do with religious traditions and are independent of established religious organizations. People can join or leave whenever they wish because there are few membership requirements.

Over a decade ago, Jim Jones' religious organization ended in a mass suicide. Many people mistakenly think Jim Jones began a cult, but actually Jonestown was a sect, firmly rooted in religious tradition. Jones appealed to people who were relatively powerless and poor. Jones worked hard in Indianapolis, Indiana with the poor and opened soup kitchens, found jobs for people, and located housing for those who were in need. Indianapolis applauded his efforts. It was only later that Jim Jones became estranged from the rest of the world.

Think about denominations, sects, or cults that are in your community or that you know about.

1. Name five denominations you recognize from your community.

    A.

   B.

   C.

   D.

   E.

2.   Now name three recognized sects.

   A.

   B.

   C.

3.   Reread about cults in your textbook. Why would Jim Jones' Jonestown NOT be considered a cult?

4. Look over your list of denominations and sects. Which churches in your lists fit the following characteristics?

A. The wealthiest:

B. Largest number of adherents:

C. Lower class:

D. Upper class:

E. Emotional zeal:

F. Highly trained clergy:

G. Loose bureaucratic organization:

H. Most supportive of the government and the status quo:

I. Sees the secular world as "evil":

CHAPTER 12
Social Change: Modernization and Social Movements

LEARNING OBJECTIVES

After reading Chapter 12, you should be able to:

1. Define social change and identify five common ways social change can occur in a society: environmental events, invasion, cultural contact, innovation, population shifts, and diffusion.

2. Discuss how change accelerates by focusing on cultural lag and the steps in the technology diffusion model.

3. Relate the cumulative model of change to modernization and the rise of the nation-state.

4. Trace the development of social change from preindustrial to the postindustrial society.

5. Explain how social change can affect personality, what effect social structure may have on personality, and examine how change affects the self.

6. Identify the factors and agents of change that influence the acceptance of social changes in a society.

7.   Discuss major forces of change: gradual or incremental change and revolutionary change.

8.   Examine Karl Marx's theory of revolution, Skocpol's modification, how revolutions can be explained and differentiate revolutionary situations, revolutionary outcomes, and revolutionary events.

9.   Explore theories of change by focusing on unidirectional and cyclical theories, the early classical two-part scheme, neoevolutionary theory, the conflict model, and a unified model of change.

10. Define collective behavior, recognize and explain the spontaneous types of collective behavior: mass hysteria, panics, rumors, and then differentiate among the types of collective behavior that reflect popular taste: crazes, fads, and fashions.

11. Characterize the nature of a public, and then examine crowd behavior, and explain the various types of crowds including: casual crowds, conventional crowds, expressive crowds, acting crowds, riots, and demonstrations.

12. List the common elements found in all crowds.

13. Present and understand three models of collective behavior, including the six necessary and sufficient conditions of the value added model.

14. Differentiate between social movements and countermovements, summarize the classification of social movements, and explain the four major phases of a social movement.

15. Review contemporary social movements, beginning with the early 1960s, and discuss how countermovements affected the goals of the movement, and then interpret the civil rights movement in the light of the resource mobilization perspective from the 1950s, through the 1960s, to the new supremacists.

GLOSSARY CONCEPTS

social change (p. 429)
environmental changes (p. 429)
invasion (p. 430)
culture contact (p. 430)
diffusion (p. 430)
innovation (p. 480)
population shifts (p. 430)
rate of change (p. 431)
cultural lag (p. 431)

adoption (p. 432)
accommodation (p. 432)
cumulative social change (p. 433)
nationalism (p. 434)
modernization (p. 436)
mobilization (p. 436)
rationality (p. 437)
postindustrial society (p. 437)
tradition-directed (p. 440)

inner-directed (p. 440)
other-directed person (p. 440)
agents of change (p. 441)
gradual or incremental change (p. 442)
revolutionary change (p. 443)
world system (p. 443)
revolutionary situation (p. 442)
unidirectional theories of evolutionary
    progress (p. 445)
cyclical theories of social change (p. 445)
neoevolutionary theory (p. 446)
conflict view of social change (p. 446)
dialectical model of social change (p. 447)
thesis (p. 447)
antithesis (p. 447)
synthesis (p. 447)
collective behavior (p. 449)
mass hysteria (p. 450)
panics (p. 450)
crazes (p. 450)
fad (p. 450)
fashions (p. 451)
rumors (p. 451)
urban legends (p. 451)
public or mass audience (p. 452)
interest group (p. 452)
crowd (p. 453)

casual crowd (p. 453)
conventional crowd (p. 453)
expressive crowd (p. 453)
acting crowds (p. 453)
mob (p. 453)
riots (p. 453)
demonstrations (p. 454)
emotional contagion model (p. 454)
value added model (p. 455)
resource mobilization model (p. 455)
social movement (p. 457)
countermovement (p. 457)
social movement organizations (p. 457)
reform movements (p. 458)
revolutionary movements (p. 458)
resistance movements (p. 459)
utopian movements (p. 459)
revolution of rising expectations (p. 459)
absolute deprivation (p. 459)
relative deprivation (p. 459)
mobilization (p. 459)
institutionalization (p. 461)
goal displacement (p. 461)
cognitive liberation (p. 465)
civil disobedience (p. 465)
populism (p. 468)

REVIEW QUESTIONS
Fill-In Questions

Fill in the blanks in the sentences below with the correct word or item.

1. Volcano eruptions and wars are examples of _____ changes. (p. 429)

2. Learning from other individuals is a source of change termed _____ _____. (p. 430)

3.   The process of new ideas, technology, or other cultural items spreading from one group, person, or society to another is _____. (p. 430)

4.   The likelihood of innovation is directly linked to the size of the _____ _____. (p. 431)

5.   The second result of technological change is _____, in which one institutional sphere undergoes internal changes in order to make more efficient use of new technology. (p. 432)

6.   In the Third World, nationalism has different meanings to various _____ _____ within the same country. (p. 434)

7.   The two aspects of sociocultural change are _____ and social differentiation. (p. 436)

8.   Modernization is linked with secularization, _____, and industrialization. (p. 436)

9.   Postindustrial societies emphasize _____ and _____ more than productive capacity and manufacturing. (p. 437)

10.   Genetic engineering is an example of _____ which has a high likelihood of accidents. (p. 438)

11.   Our sense of self and our position in the _____ _____ are mutually reinforcing. (p. 440)

12.   The _____ - directed person scans the environment for appropriate messages to guide behavior. (p. 440)

13.   One difference between colonialism and the post colonial world is that the raw materials from less developed nations must now be _____ for. (pp. 443 and 444)

14.   Today, revolutions are thought to arise from _____ in the social structure, rather than being deliberately planned. (p. 444)

15.   The movement of birth cohorts and their flow through the social system are important factors of _____ change. (p. 444)

16.   Conflict theory completes the functional and neoevolutionary views of change because it specifies the _____ and the processes of change in the social system. (p. 446)

17.   The forces of opposition for Marx were the _____. (p. 447)

18.   The new social order that comes from the conflict between the thesis and the antithesis Marx called the _____ . (p. 447)

19.   To synthesize the neoevolutionary and the conflict models of change, general change best can be explained in terms of changes in the _____ _____ of society. (p. 447)

20.   _____, _____, and _____ _____ are forms of collective behavior which are short-lived, relatively spontaneous, lacking in clear-cut goals, and expressive. (p. 450)

21.   Today, _____ _____ is a form of collective behavior which typically involves women and children who quickly perform simple, repetitive jobs. (p. 450)

22.   To a young child, a Teenage Mutant Ninja Turtle figure, Nintendo, and a Bart Simpson sweatshirt would involve a(n) _____. (p. 450)

23.   Adorning the body carries important information about an individual's_____ in all types of societies. (p. 451)

24.   All kinds of advertising are designed to create a(n) _____ for a given product. (p. 452)

25.   A temporary gathering brought together by some common concern or activity is a(n) _____. (p. 453)

26.   People strolling through a shopping mall admiring store displays are part of a(n) _____ crowd. (p. 453)

27.   People attending a movie premier are part of a(n) _____ crowd. (p. 453)

28.   _____ _____ are the main way people are recruited to collective activities. (p. 456)

29.   _____ _____ _____ are specific formal organizations, like the Ku Klux Klan, that channel discontent into concrete actions. (p. 457)

30.   The three variables used to describe a specific social movement include: tactics, depth of change, and _____ _____. (p. 458)

31. _____ movements seek fundamental changes in norms and institutions. (p. 458)

32. The type of social movement apt to resort to violence is the _____ movement. (pp. 458, 459)

33. The New Christian Right is an example of a(n) _____ movement which seeks to stop change and to restore "traditional" values. (p. 459)

34. In phase _____ of a social movement, widespread unrest is linked to a condition in society. (p. 459)

35. _____ deprivation is a lack of basic necessities but _____ deprivation happens when people feel unfairly treated in comparison to others thought to be their equals. (p. 459)

36. The mobilization of resources occurs in phase _____ of a social movement. (p. 459)

37. Success of a social movement takes the form of _____, when beliefs are accepted and goals are embodied in stable organizations. (p. 461)

38. The partial success of a social movement creates problems of maintaining _____ _____. (p. 461)

39. Two basic strategies agents of social control may use are _____ or _____. (p. 461)

40. Of all the social movements of the 1960s, the one that was easiest to control involved _____. (p. 464)

41. _____ movement advocates are most frequently ridiculed. (p. 464)

42. The goal of the civil rights movement was primarily _____. (p. 466)

43. Skinheads and other supremacist groups embrace an old idea known as _____, or a grass-roots social movement that combines antibusiness feelings with racial, religious, and ethnic intolerance. (p. 468)

True-False Questions

*Circle **T** if the statement is true. Circle **F** if the statement is false.*

T   F   1.   When a country is overrun by another, the type of change involved is called invasion. (p. 430)

T   F   2.   Technology is the most easily diffused item. (p. 431)

T   F   3.   When innovations are accepted by people in a society, the group increases its cultural base. (p. 431)

T   F   4.   The social institutions of a society become more complex as societies become more intricate. (p. 433)

T   F   5.   The notion of a nation-state as a separate political unit and a source of group loyalty is a new idea. (p. 434)

T   F   6.   Nationalism has quickly developed in African countries. (p. 434)

T   F   7.   For Third World nations, the common element in nationalism is shared culture. (p. 434)

T   F   8.   Change within any society is toward increasing complexity. (p. 436)

T   F   9.   The inner-directed person may experience anxiety as the self is constantly constructed and reconstructed to fit various roles and statuses. (pp. 440, 441)

T   F   10.   Change is promoted or restricted by people who occupy statuses in social systems. (p. 441)

T   F   11.   Marx argued in favor of a general theory of revolution. (p. 443)

T   F   12.   The political structure, rather than the social class structure, changes in the industrial societies which undergo revolution. (p. 443)

T   F   13.   Most peripheral societies have a raw material badly needed by modern industrial societies. (pp. 443, 444)

T   F   14.   The effects of a revolutionary event can vary by time and place. (p. 445)

T   F   15.   Cyclical theories of social change have great predictive value. (p. 445)

T   F   16.   Neoevolutionary theory assumes that some societies progress at a superior rate than others. (p. 446)

T   F   17.   Change outside the society best can be analyzed in terms of class-based interests. (p. 448)

T   F   18.   Collective behavior occurs randomly. (p. 450)

T   F   19.   Fads may be more enduring than fashions and involve more socially significant trends. (p. 451)

T   F   20.   Urban legends involve rumors that resonate to deeply held fears regarding aspects of life beyond personal control. (p. 451)

T   F   21.   A crowd is a type of group because it has a structure. (p. 453)

T   F   22.   An acting crowd can easily become a mob. (p. 453)

T   F   23.   Riots are more spontaneous than mobs. (p. 453)

T   F   24.   How acting crowds are perceived depends on who is involved in them. (p. 453)

T   F   25.   A crucial factor in demonstrations is the size of the crowd. (p. 454)

T   F   26.   People in crowds are suggestible. (p. 454)

T   F   27.   Structural strain involves preconditions built into society's structure which contribute to collective behaviors. (p. 455)

T   F   28.   The resource mobilization model views protests as abnormally occurring events that operate outside the ongoing processes of society. (p. 455)

T   F   29.   A modification of the resource mobilization model involves including social-psychological variables. (p. 456)

T   F   30.   Network pressure to join a collective effort can operate despite an individual's attitudes. (p. 457)

T   F   31.   Relative deprivation leads to withdrawal from collective action because of profound feelings of hopelessness. (p. 459)

T   F   32.   Leaders emerge in the development of a social movement during phase two. (p. 459)

T   F   33.   The success of a social movement is determined by its goals. (p. 461)

T   F   34.   The civil rights movement is dealing with a public perception that its goals have been met. (p. 461)

T   F   35.   Goal displacement is a major danger in a social movement becoming success-fully organized. (p. 461)

T   F   36.   Cognitive liberation occurs when the idea of collective protest can be seriously considered. (p. 465)

T   F   37.   The first civil rights protest activities were spontaneous and violent. (p. 466)

T   F   38.   The Ku Klux Klan and the American Nazis are right wing groups. (p. 467)

T   F   39.   Membership in new supremacist groups is actually quite small. (p. 467)

T   F   40.   The opinions of the Ku Klux Klan and the American Nazi Party are new to our society. (pp. 467, 468)

Matching Questions

Match the items in Column B with the correct answer in Column A (columns continue on next page).

COLUMN A	COLUMN B
1. agents of change (p. 441)	a. A type of social action in which the traditional and emotional bases for behavior are replaced by belief in a logical relationship between means and ends.
2. gradual or incremental change (p. 442)	
3. revolutionary events (pp. 444, 445)	b. Change that takes place along a single path and was a popular theory in late nineteenth century England.
4. social change (p. 429)	c. A social process through which a society becomes more internally differentiated and complex, and in which science and technology guide change.
5. inner-directed person (p. 440)	
6. cultural lag (p. 431)	d. Defined by its capacity to handle and transmit information.
7. common ways change occurs (pp. 429, 430)	e. Diffusion, innovation, population shifts, invasion, cultural contact, environmental events.
8. postindustrial society (p. 437)	f. Discovery and invention.
9. revolutionary outcome (p. 444)	g. One set of power holders is displaced by another.
10. world system (p. 443)	h. The process through which values, norms, institutions, social relationships, and stratification systems alter over time.
11. rationality (p. 437)	i. The first result of technological change where people substitute the new technology for an old one.
12. innovation (p. 430)	
13. adoption (p. 432)	j. The economic and political relationships among industrial and less-developed societies.
14. modernization (p. 436)	k. People who occupy statuses through which they can influence the direction of change.
15. unidirectional change (p. 445)	l. The tendency for parts of culture to change and adapt at different rates after the introduction of a new technology.
16. civil disobedience (p. 466)	
17. mobilization (p. 459)	m. Change that involves a long process and which may go unnoticed.
18. social movements (p. 457)	n. The worker in an industrial society would be an example.

COLUMN A	COLUMN B

<table>
<tr><td>19.</td><td>public or mass audience (p. 452)</td><td>o.</td><td>The model that focuses on how the intensity of crowds develop.</td></tr>
<tr><td>20.</td><td>demonstrations (p. 454)</td><td>p.</td><td>Actions caused by a sudden overwhelming need to escape danger.</td></tr>
<tr><td>21.</td><td>rumors (p. 451)</td><td>q.</td><td>Unconfirmed information, which may or may not be correct.</td></tr>
<tr><td>22.</td><td>utopian movements (p. 459)</td><td>r.</td><td>These involve large numbers of people mobilized to promote or resist social and cultural change.</td></tr>
<tr><td>23.</td><td>emotional contagion model (p. 454)</td><td>s.</td><td>This model stresses the supports available to protesters, as well as the tactics used by social control agents.</td></tr>
<tr><td>24.</td><td>panics (p. 450)</td><td>t.</td><td>Involves peaceful refusal to obey unjust laws in the name of a higher morality.</td></tr>
<tr><td>25.</td><td>resource mobilization model (p. 455)</td><td>u.</td><td>These movements aim for an ideal society for a select group of true believers.</td></tr>
<tr><td></td><td></td><td>v.</td><td>This stage of a social movement occurs when members gain the resources required to create an organization, active participation, and social tolerance for its existence.</td></tr>
<tr><td></td><td></td><td>w.</td><td>The only type of collective behavior where people are not in the same place at the same time, but who relate similarly to particular issues.</td></tr>
<tr><td></td><td></td><td>x.</td><td>Highly organized acting crowds with a clearly defined goal.</td></tr>
</table>

ANSWERS
Answers to Fill-In Questions

1.	environmental	15.	unplanned	30.	goal state
2.	culture contact	16.	sources	31.	reform
3.	diffusion	17.	antithesis	32.	revolutionary
4.	culture base	18.	synthesis	33.	resistance
5.	accommodation	19.	economic base	34.	one
6.	social classes	20.	fads; panics; mass hysteria	35.	absolute; relative
7.	mobilization	21.	mass hysteria	36.	three
8.	urbanization	22.	craze	37.	institutionalization
9.	science; technology	23.	status	38.	members' commitment
		24.	public	39.	repression; cooptation
10.	biotechnology	25.	crowd	40.	students
11.	social structure	26.	casual	41.	women's
12.	other	27.	conventional	42.	reformist
13.	paid	28.	interpersonal contacts	43.	populism
14.	strains	29.	social movement organizations		

Answers to True-False Questions

1.	T	11.	F	21.	F	31.	F
2.	T	12.	T	22.	T	32.	T
3.	T	13.	F	23.	F	33.	F
4.	F	14.	T	24.	T	34.	T
5.	T	15.	F	25.	T	35.	T
6.	F	16.	F	26.	T	36.	T
7.	F	17.	F	27.	F	37.	F
8.	F	18.	F	28.	F	38.	T
9.	F	19.	F	29.	T	39.	T
10.	T	20.	T	30.	T	40.	F

Answers to Matching Questions

1.	k	8.	d	15.	b	22.	u
2.	m	9.	g	16.	t	23.	o
3.	x	10.	j	17.	v	24.	p
4.	h	11.	a	18.	r	25.	s
5.	n	12.	f	19.	w		
6.	l	13.	i	20.	x		
7.	e	14.	c	21.	q		

EXERCISE #1

Many of the nations of the Middle East have undergone changes. Choose one nation from this region.

1.   List the sources of change for your nation.

2.   Describe the rate of change by reviewing two newspaper sources or a library source which describes your country.

3.   What evidence do you find for cultural lag? Accommodation?

4.   What trends have there been for nationalism? Describe them.

5.   Which theory of social change best describes changes in the nation you selected? Discuss how the theory fits your observation.

EXERCISE #2

You may be part of different crowds on a daily basis. Select one of these crowds. You will want to reread pages 453-454.

1.   What type of crowd were you part of?

2.   Why or for what purpose was this crowd formed?

3.   Analyze your crowd using either the value added model or resource mobilization and explain how your crowd came to be and what happened with it.